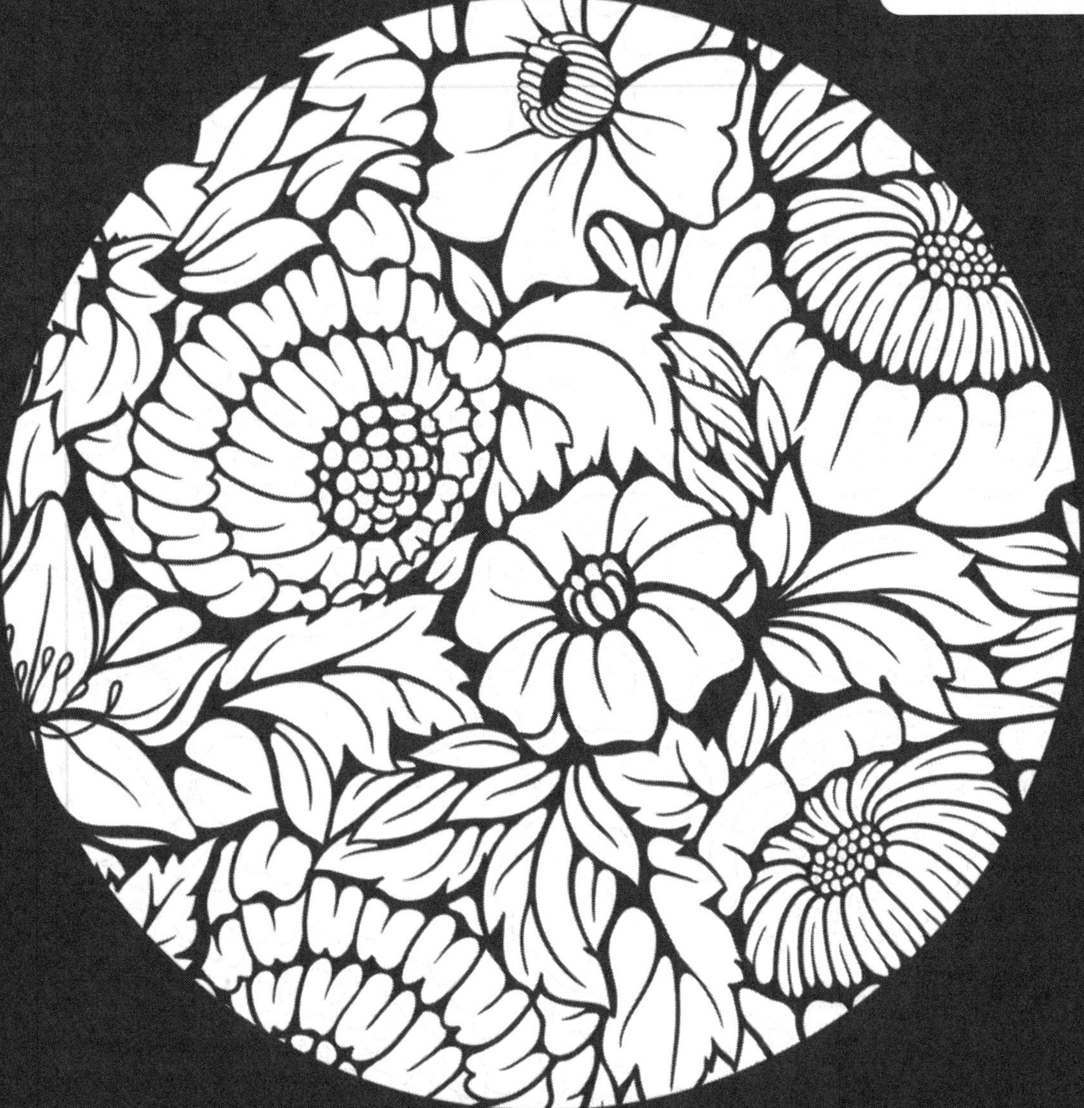

Coloring Book For Seniors

Anti-Stress Designs Vol 1

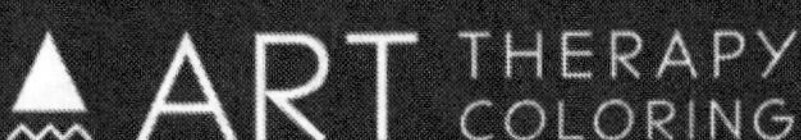

Preview of Coloring Pages

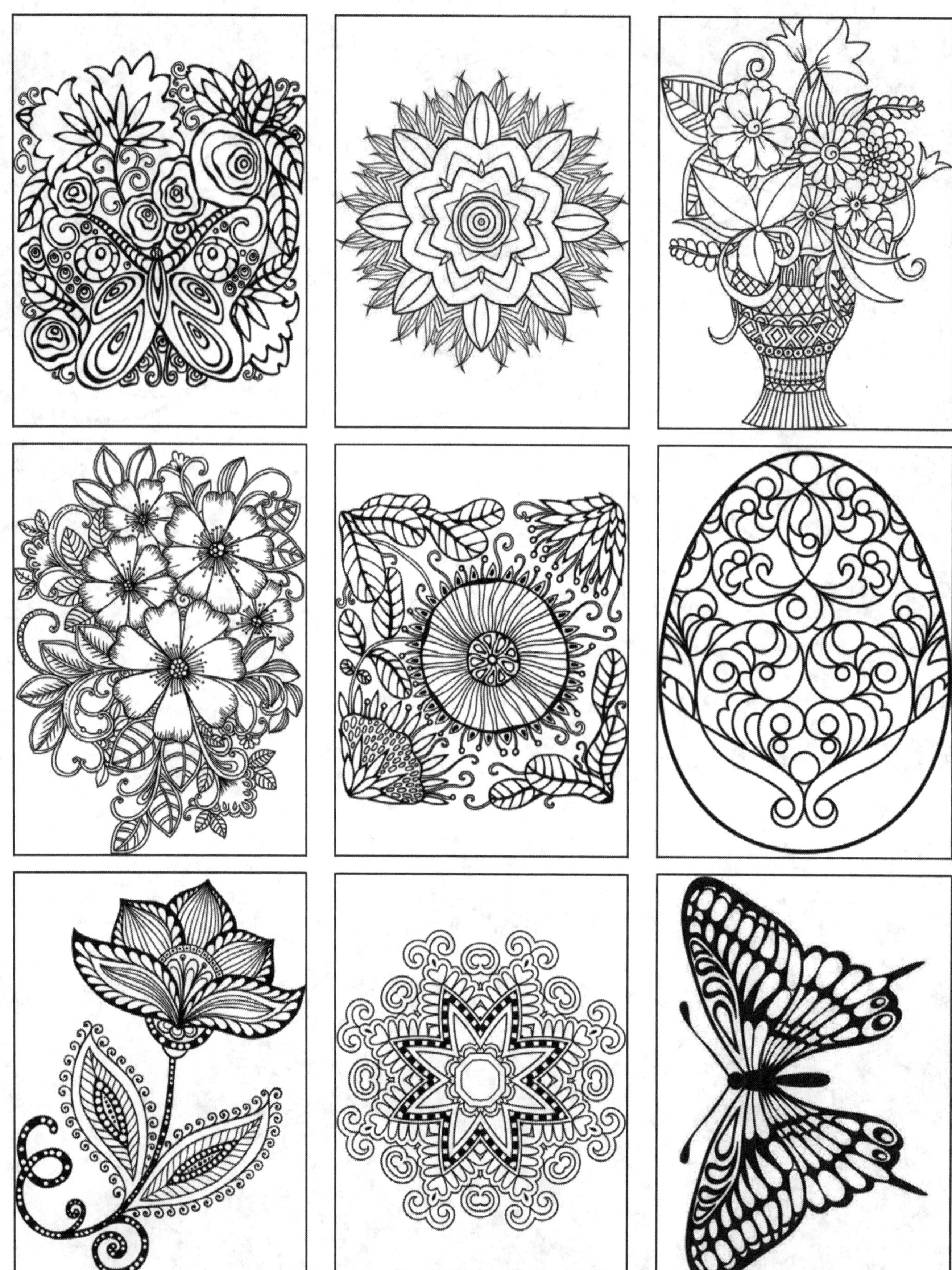

www.arttherapycoloring.com

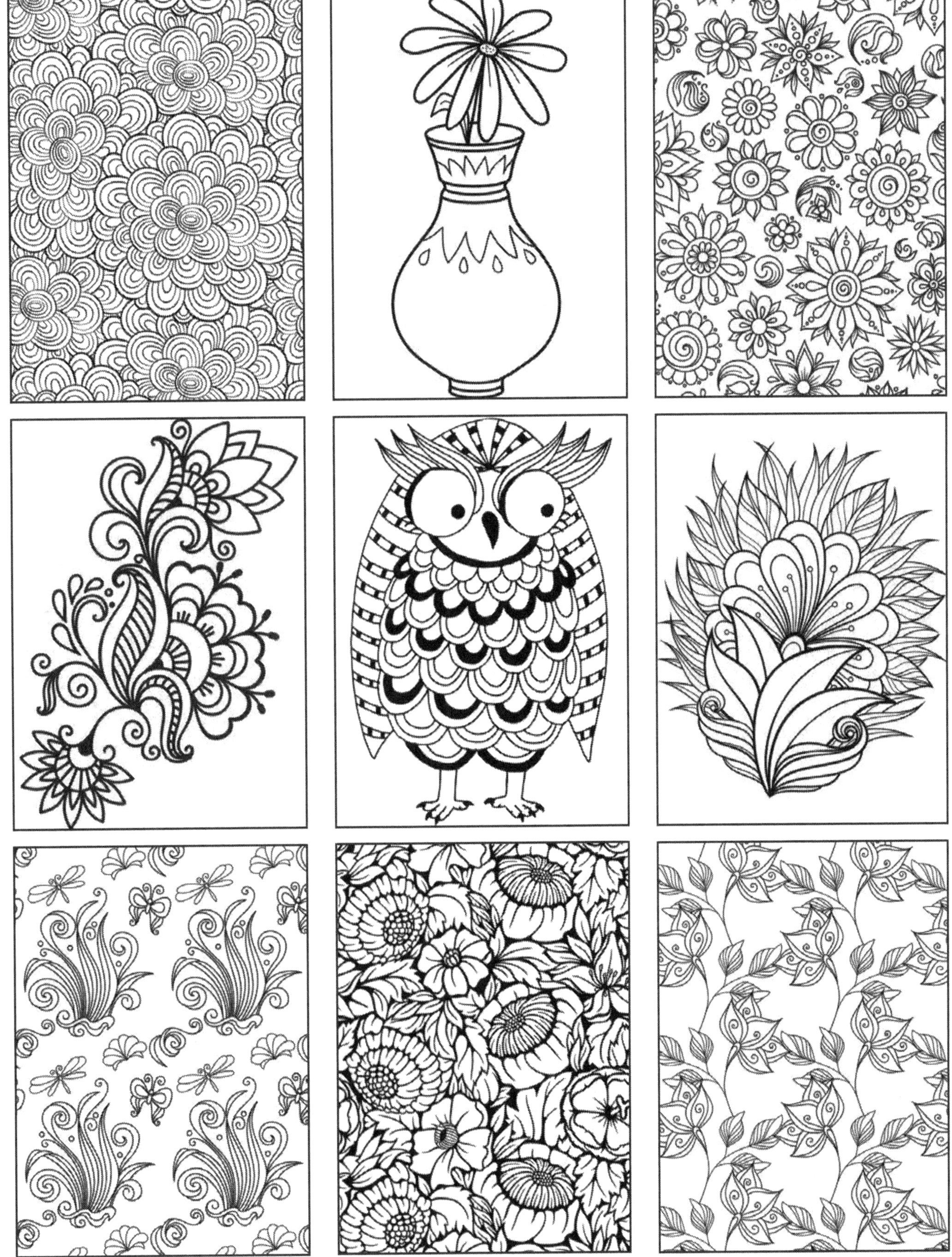

Preview of Coloring Pages

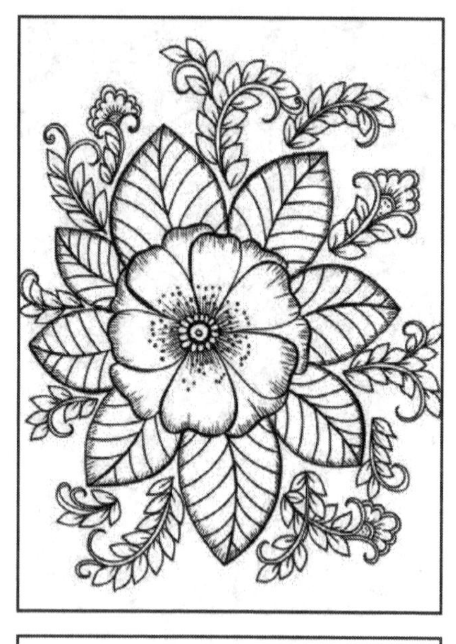
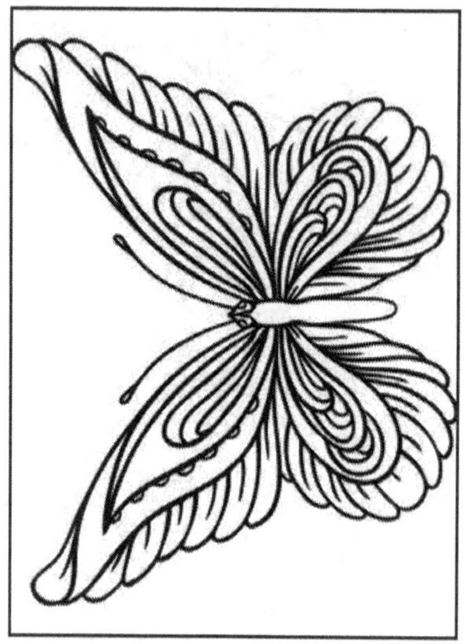
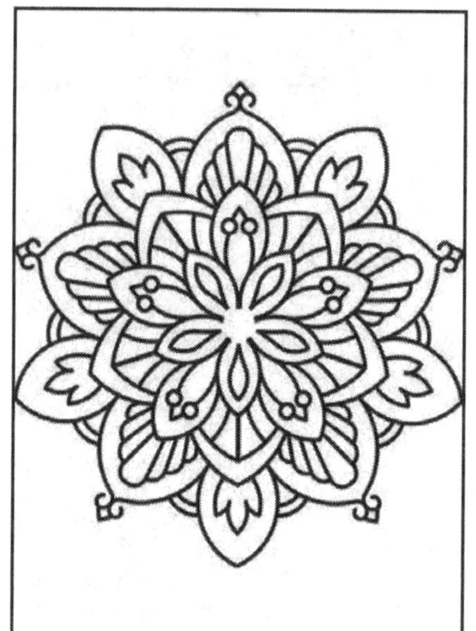
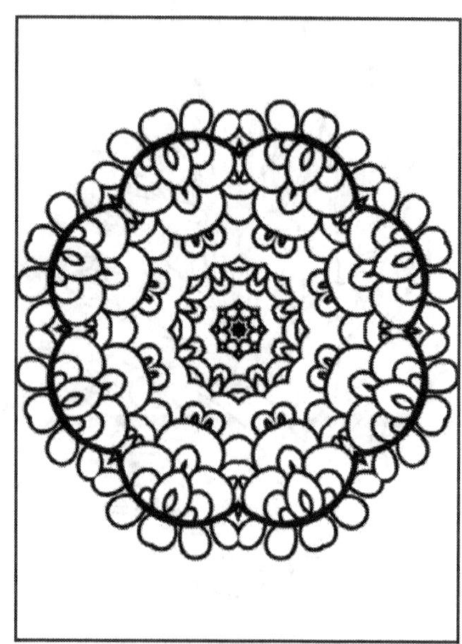
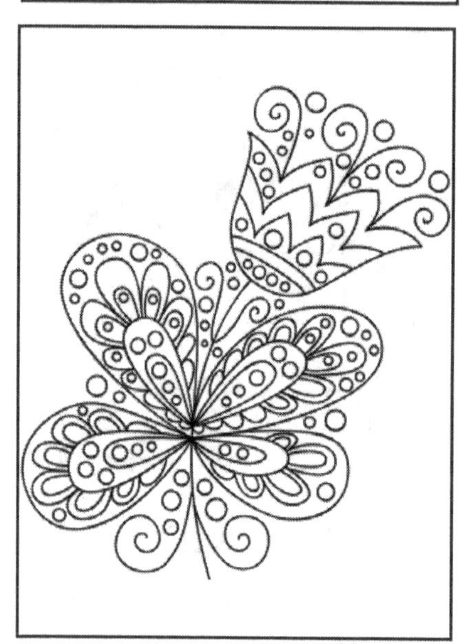
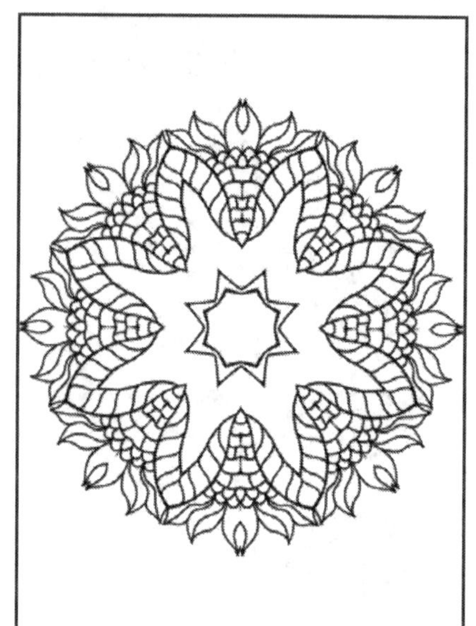
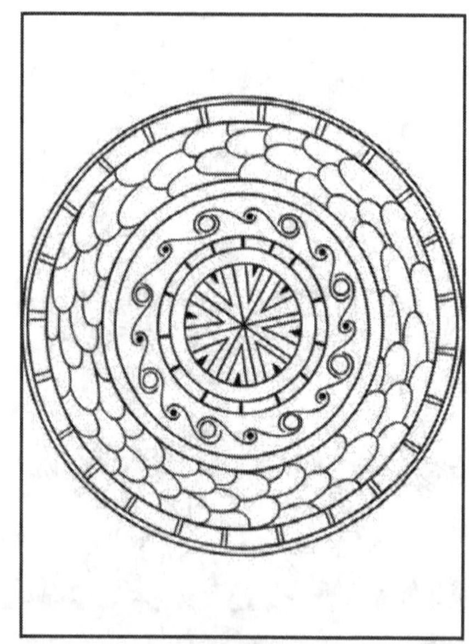
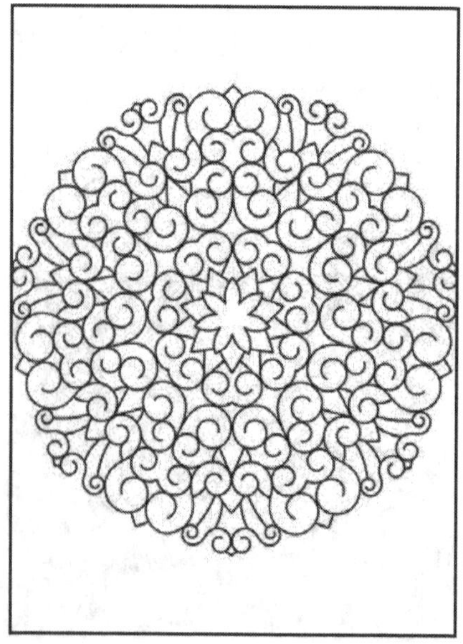
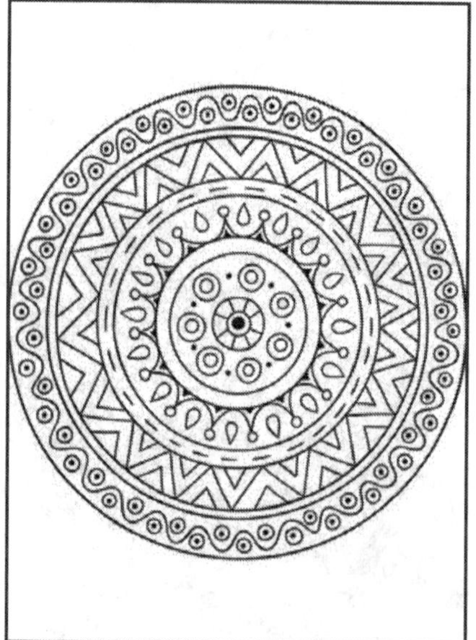

www.arttherapycoloring.com

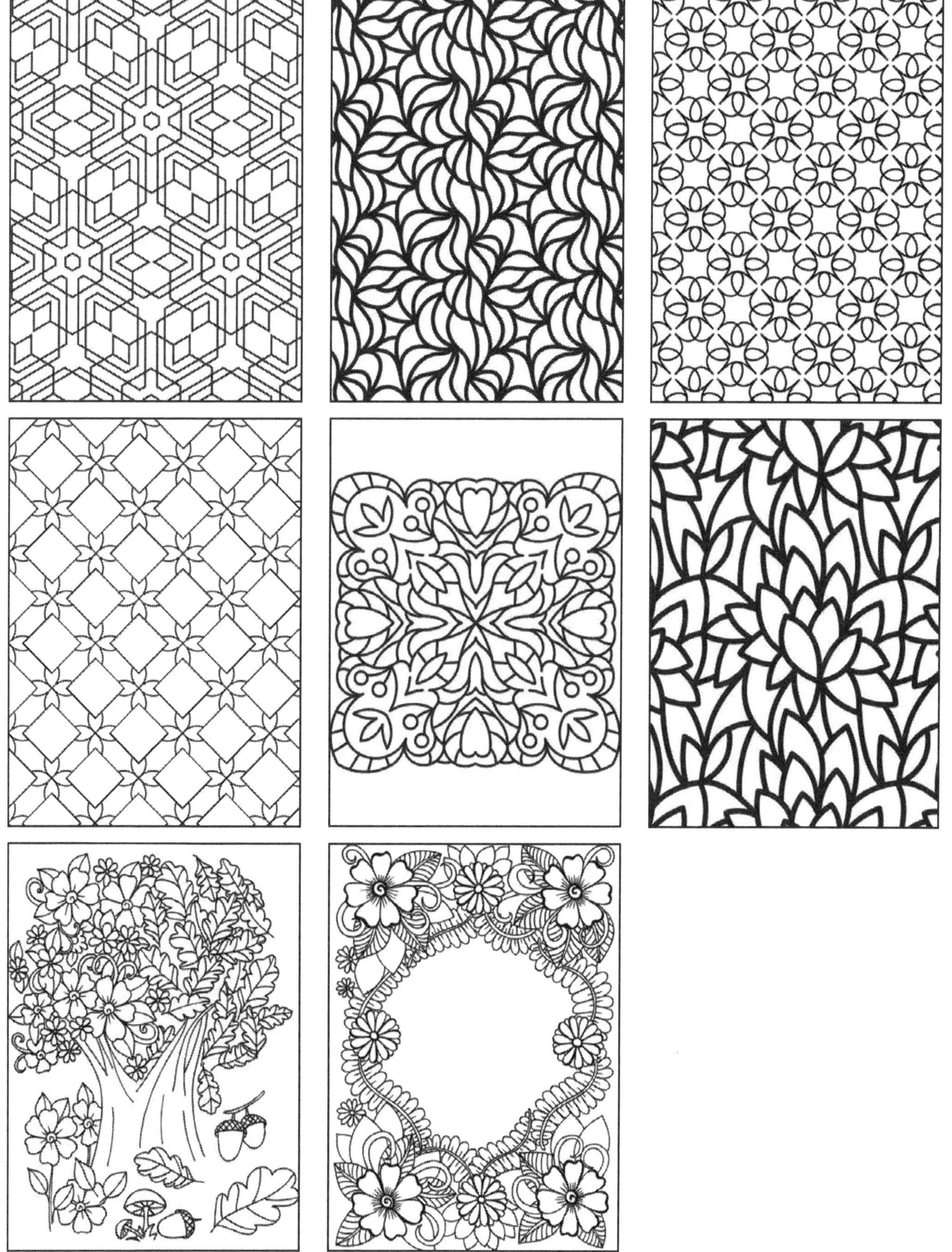

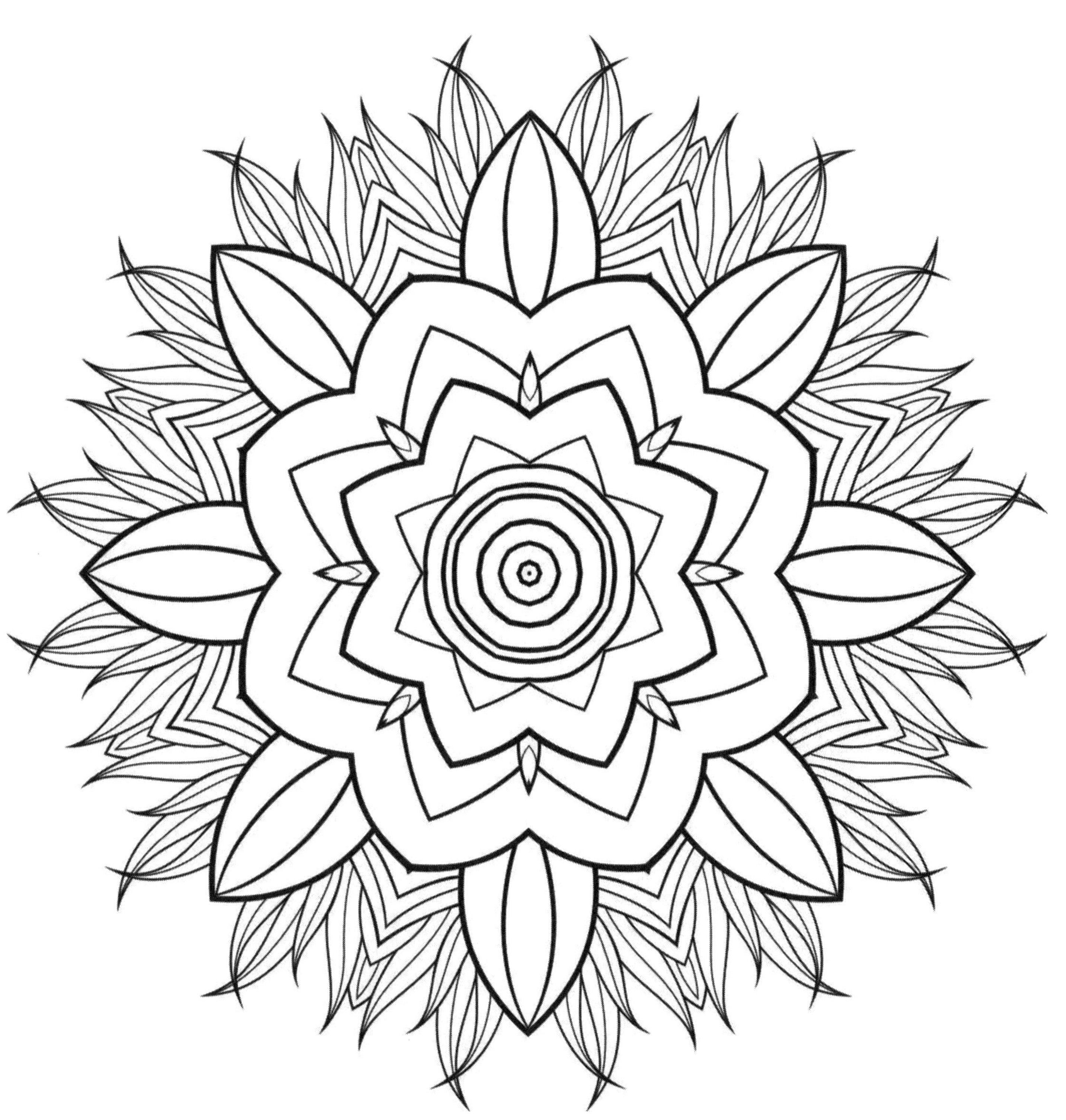

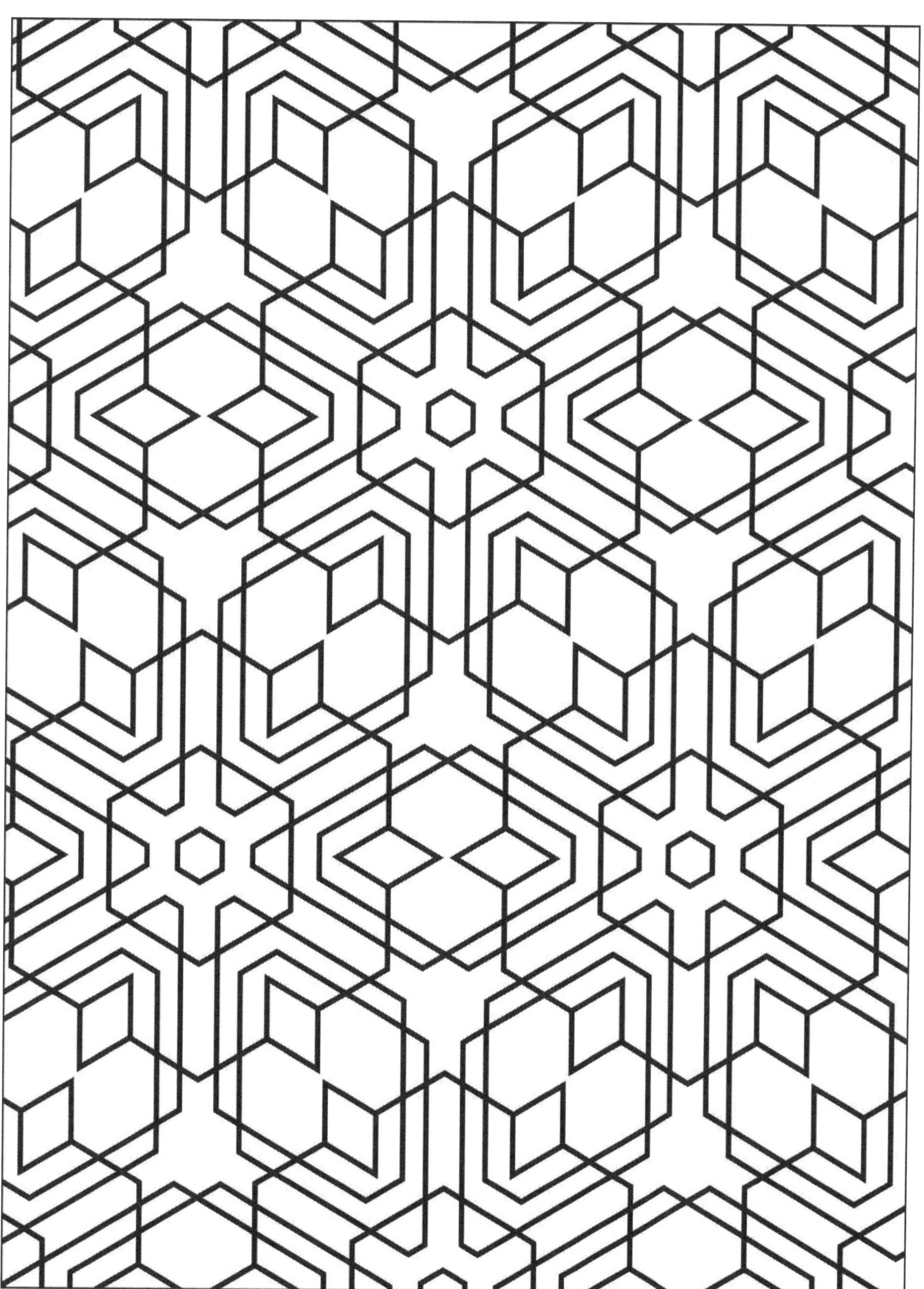

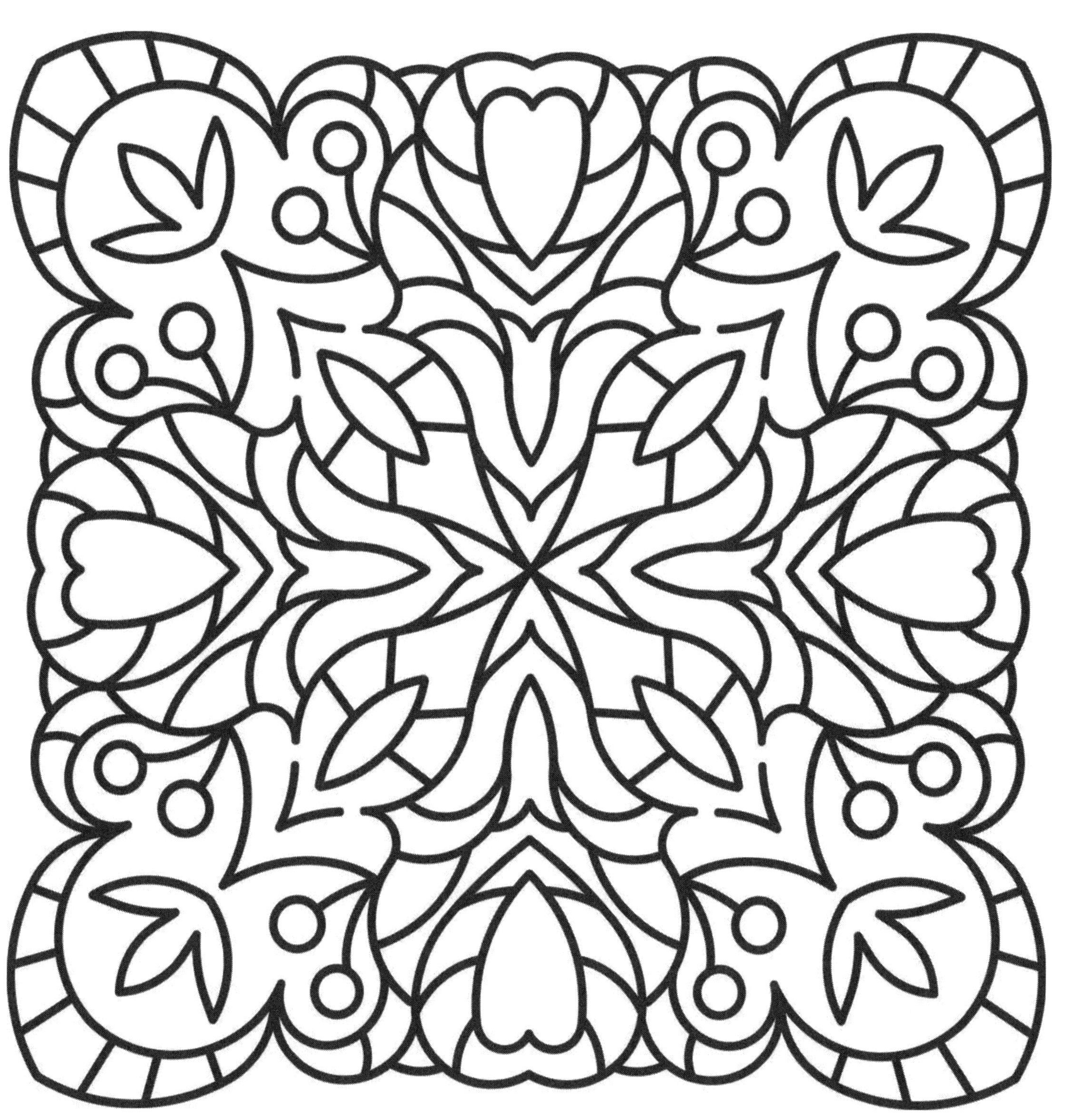

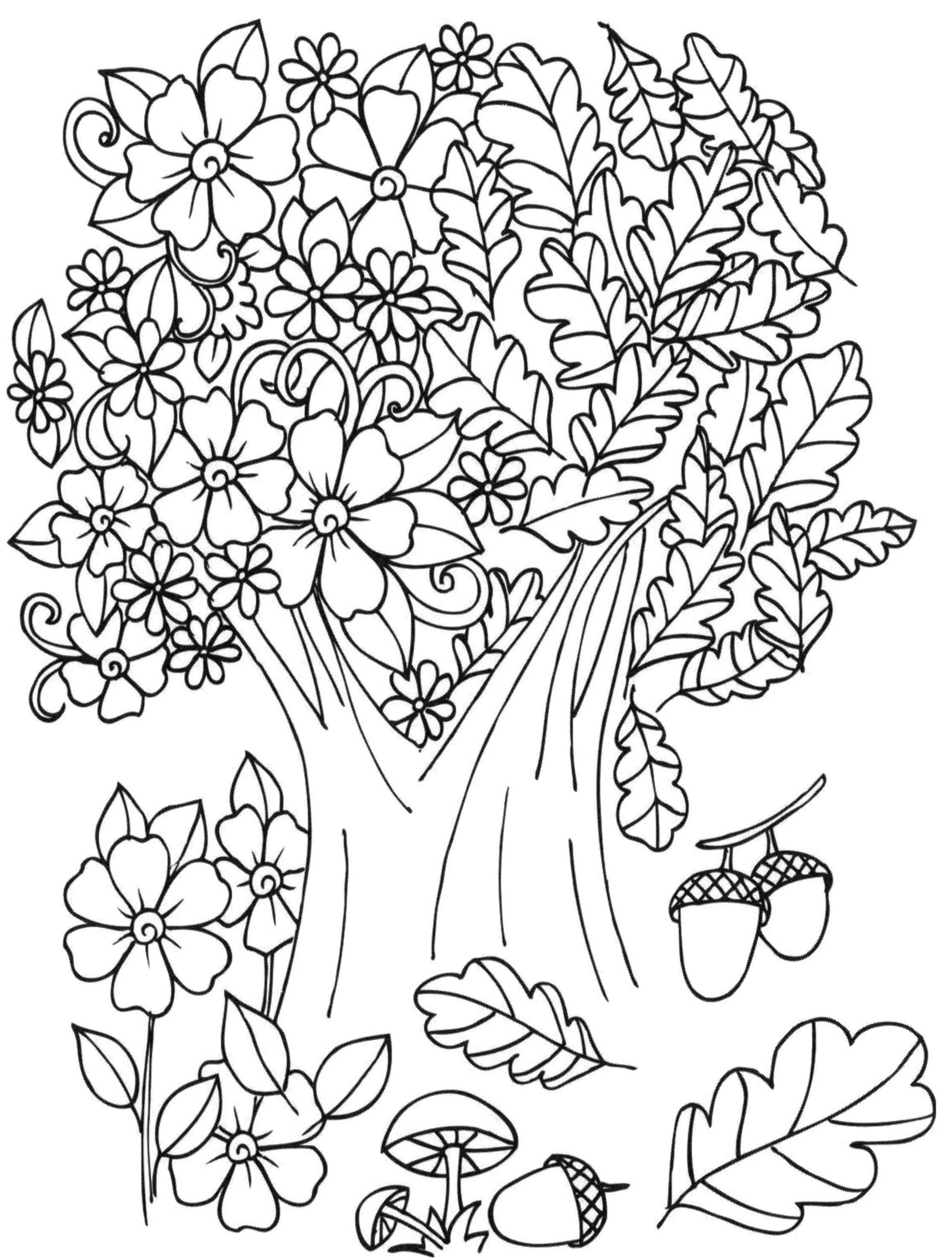

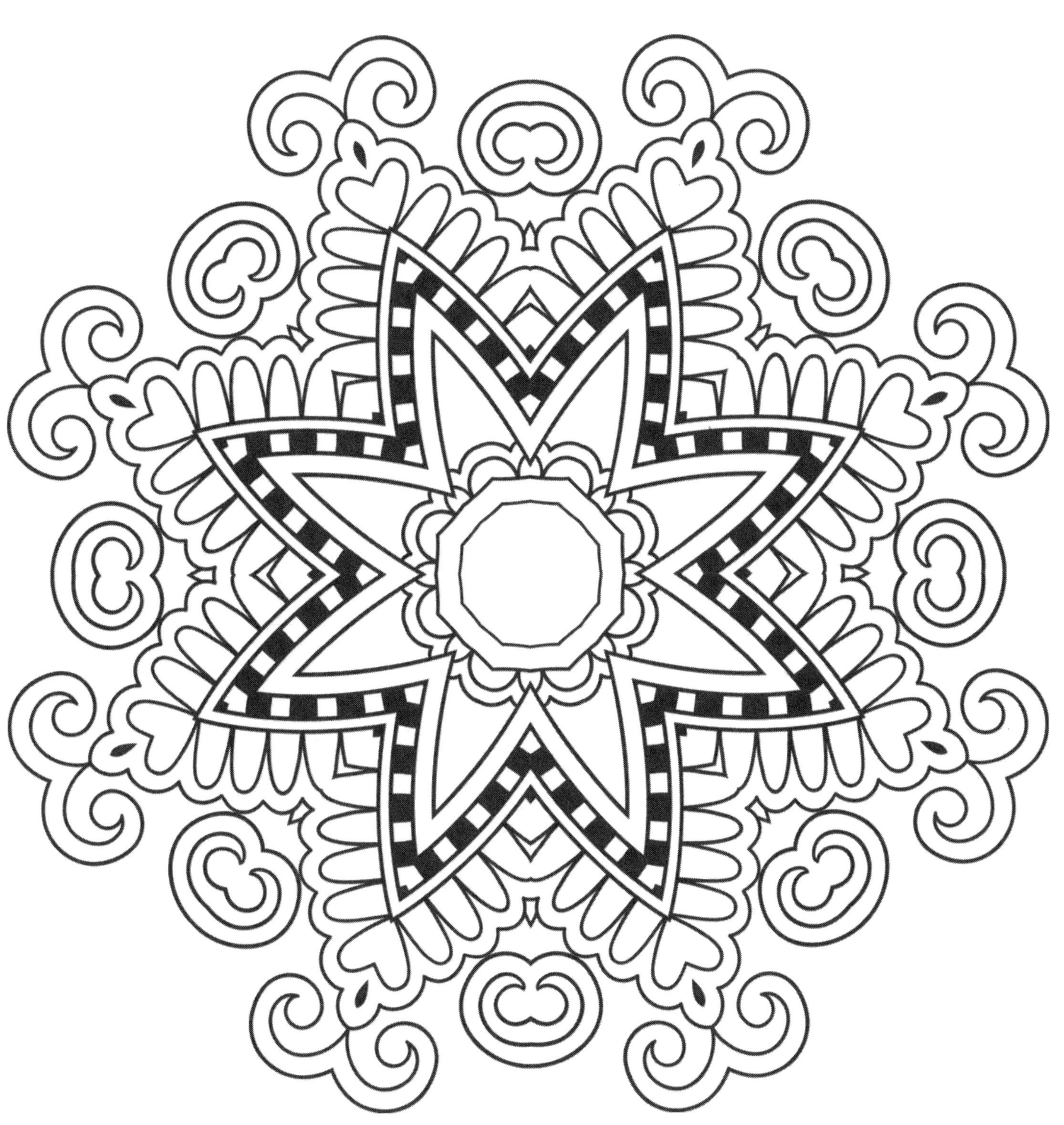

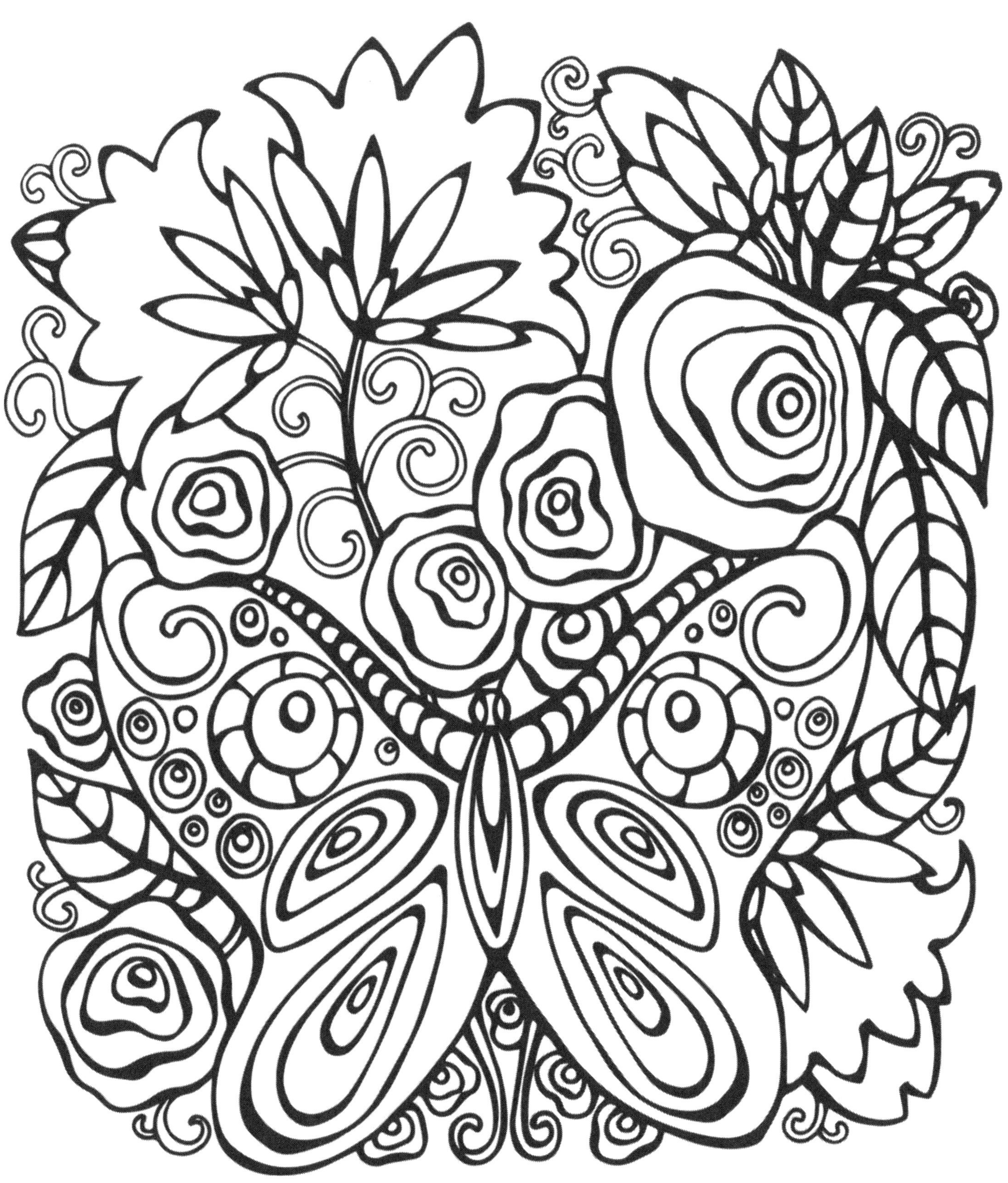

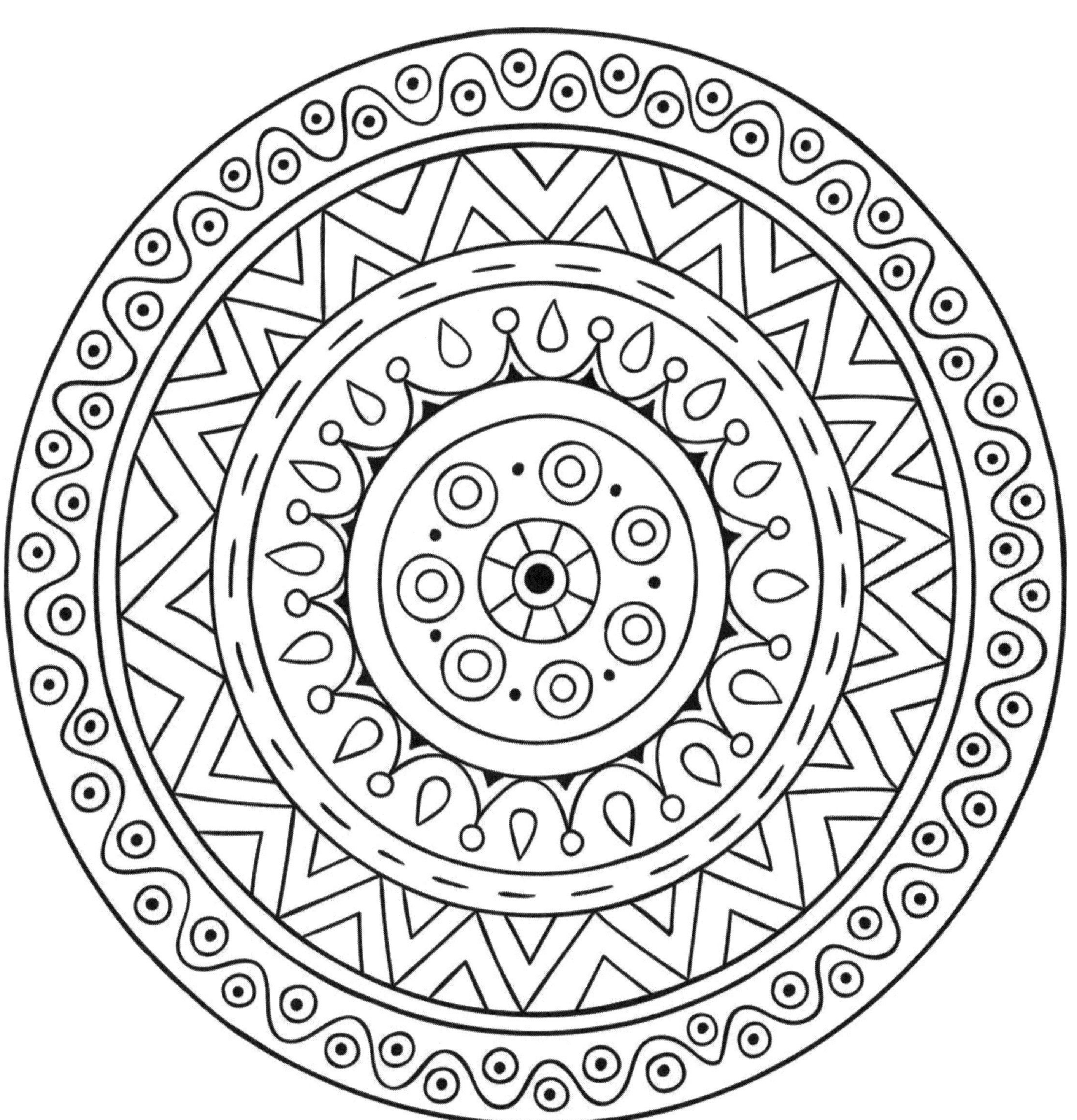

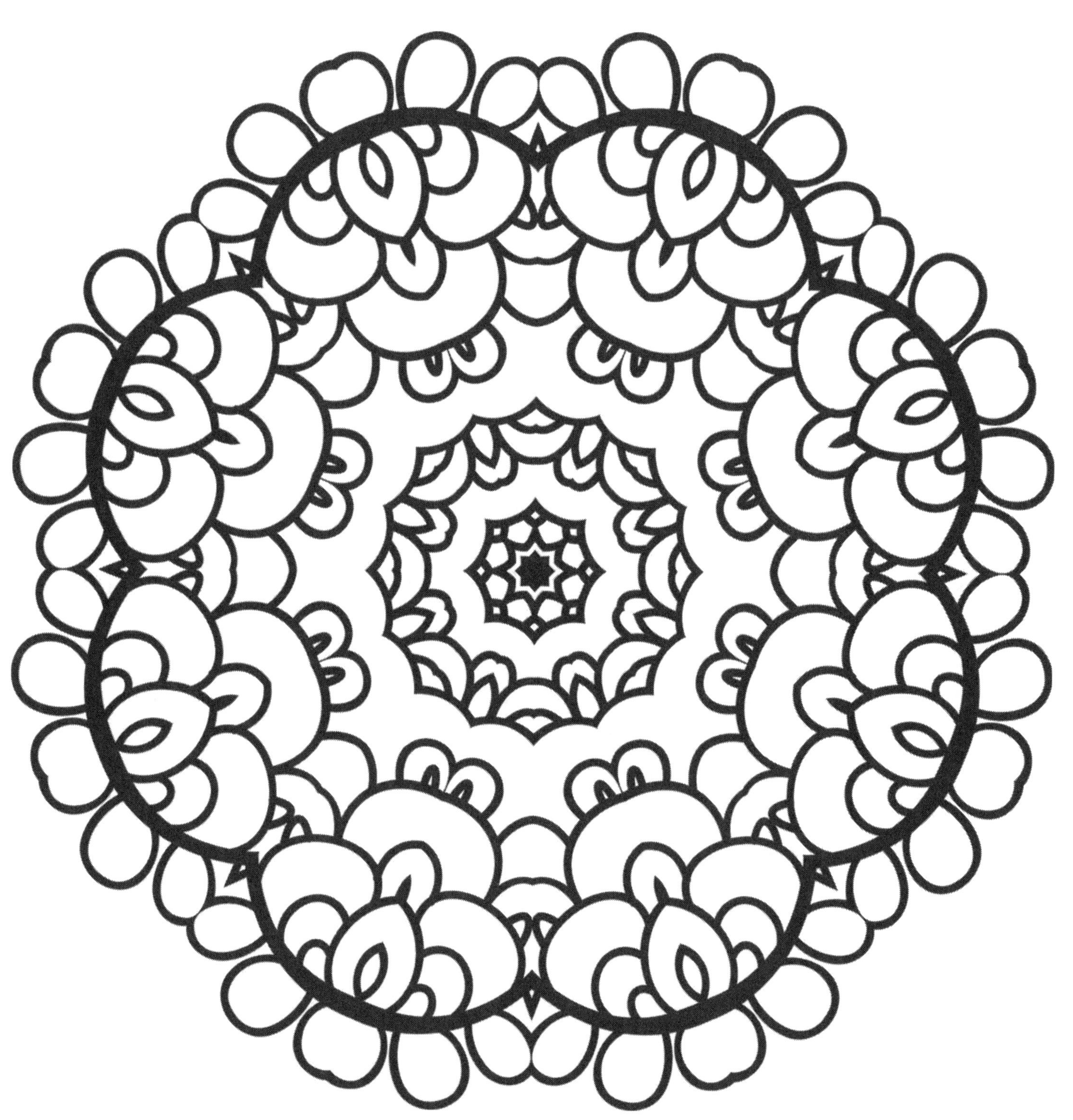

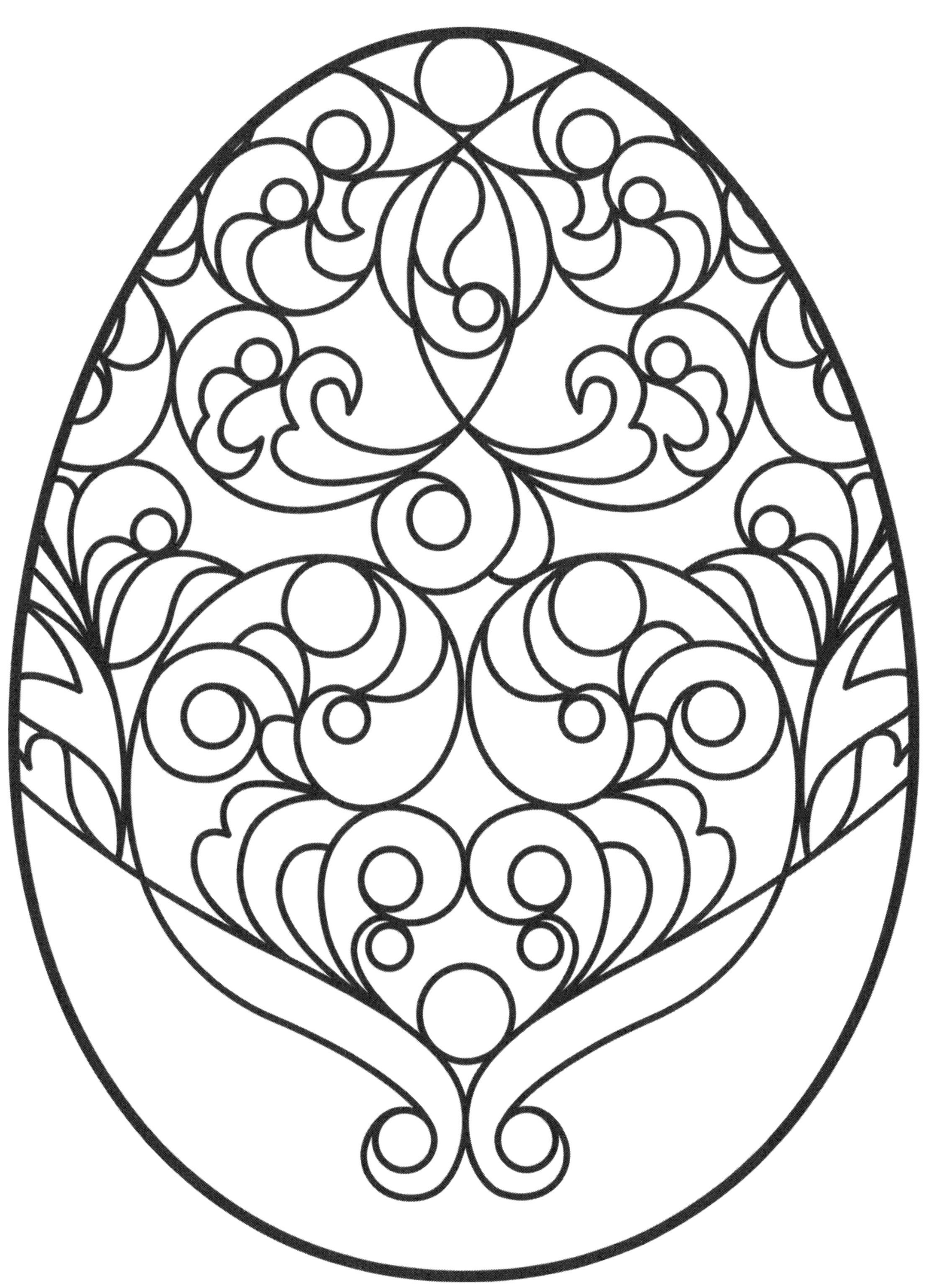

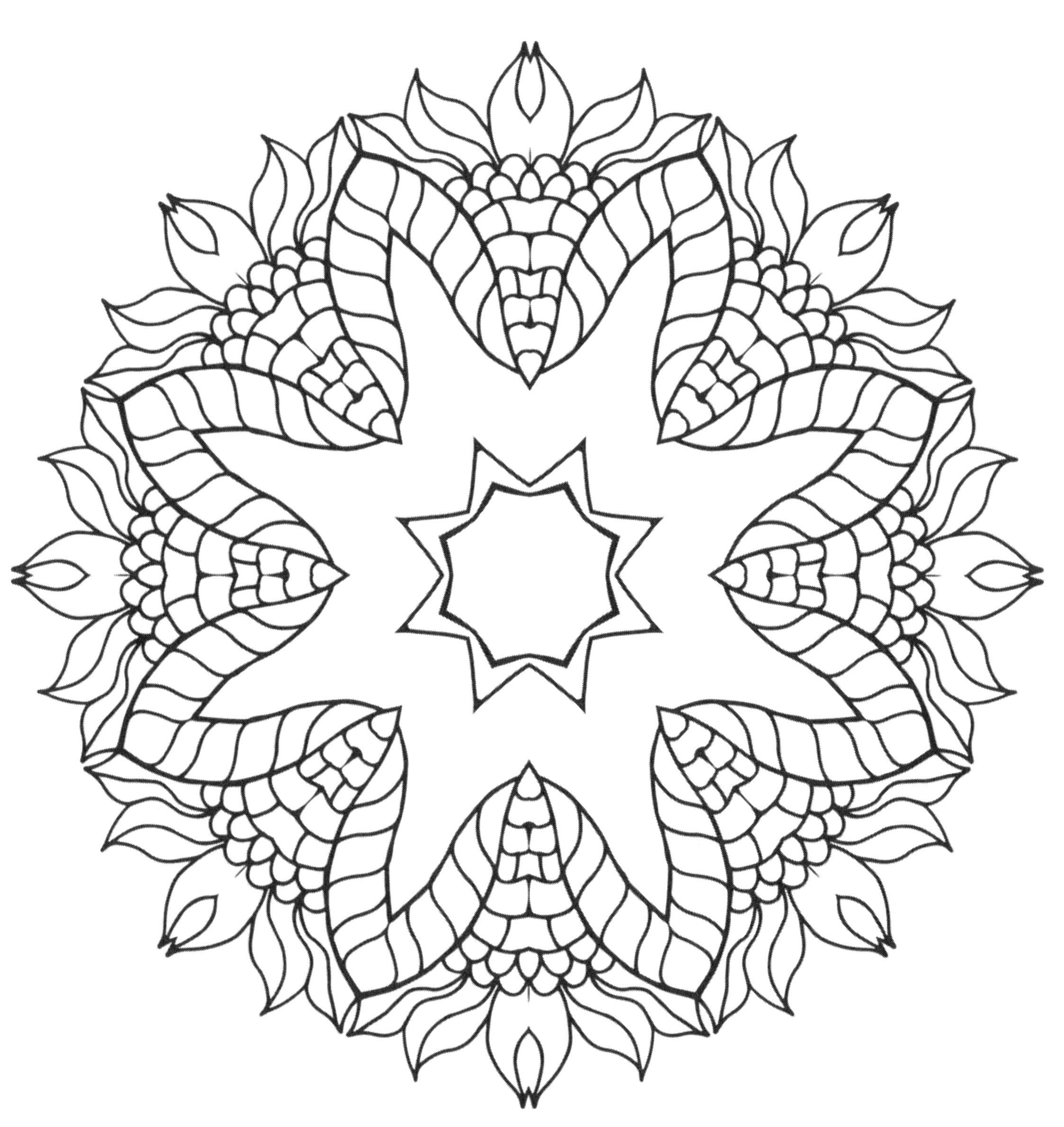

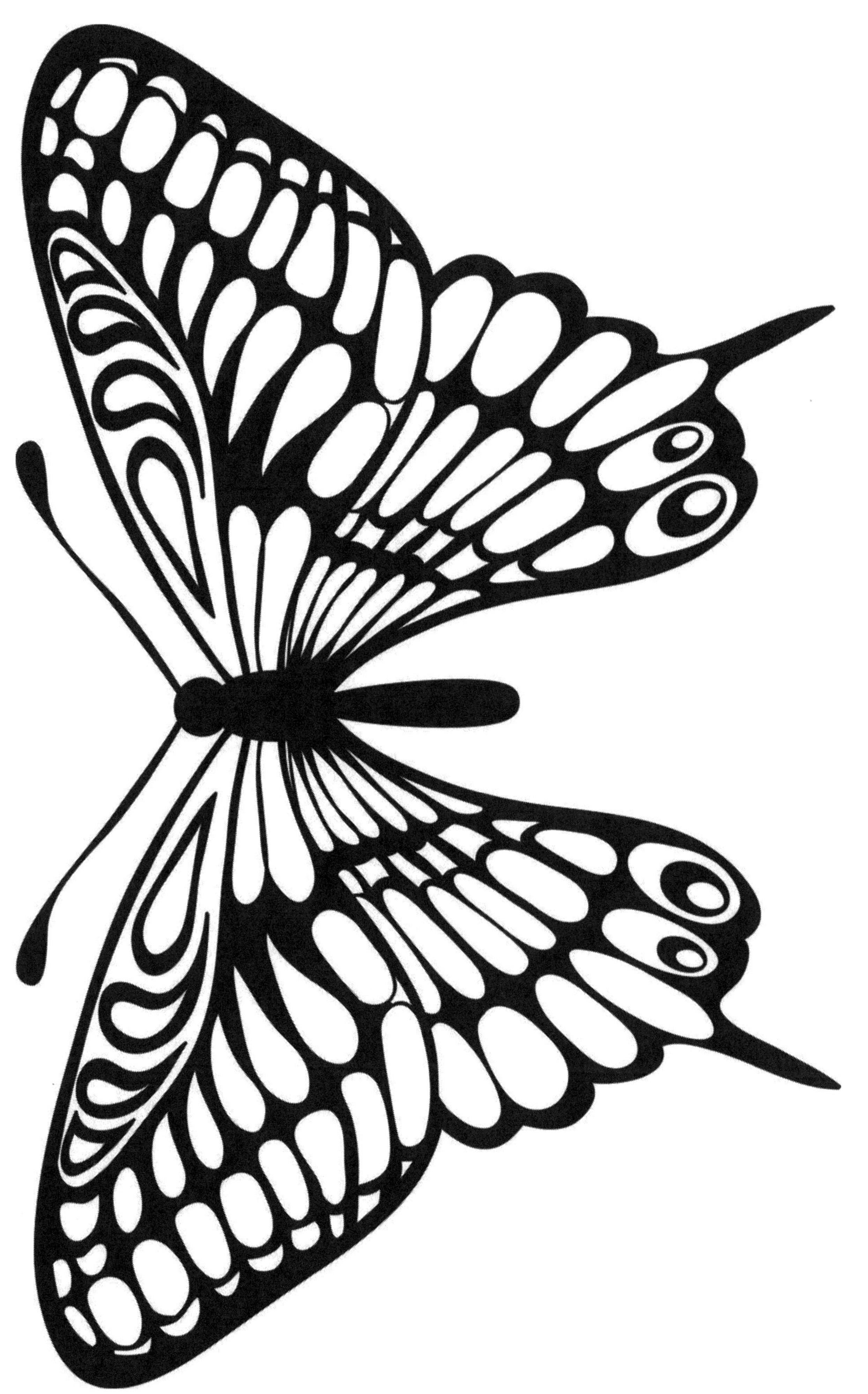

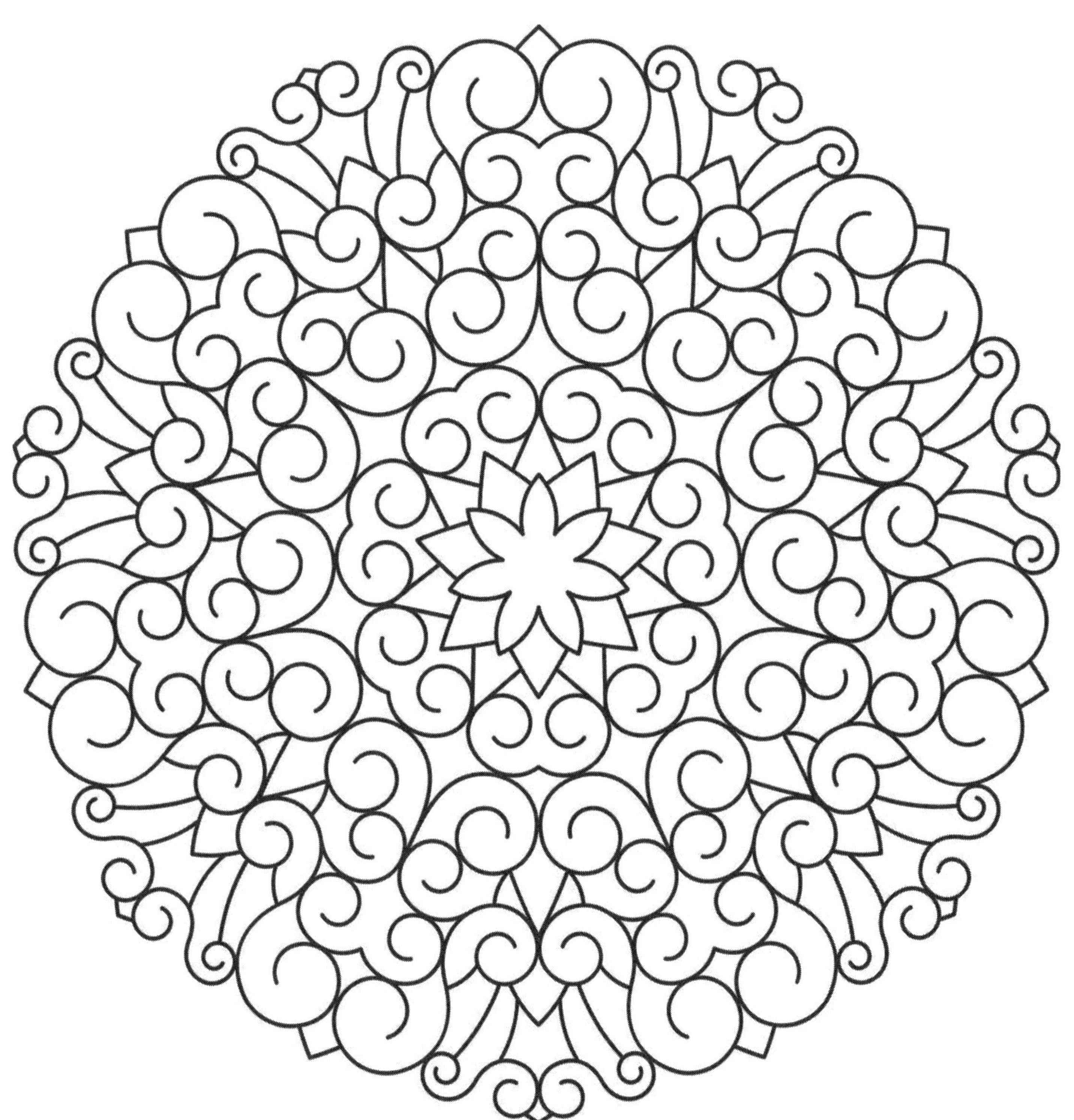

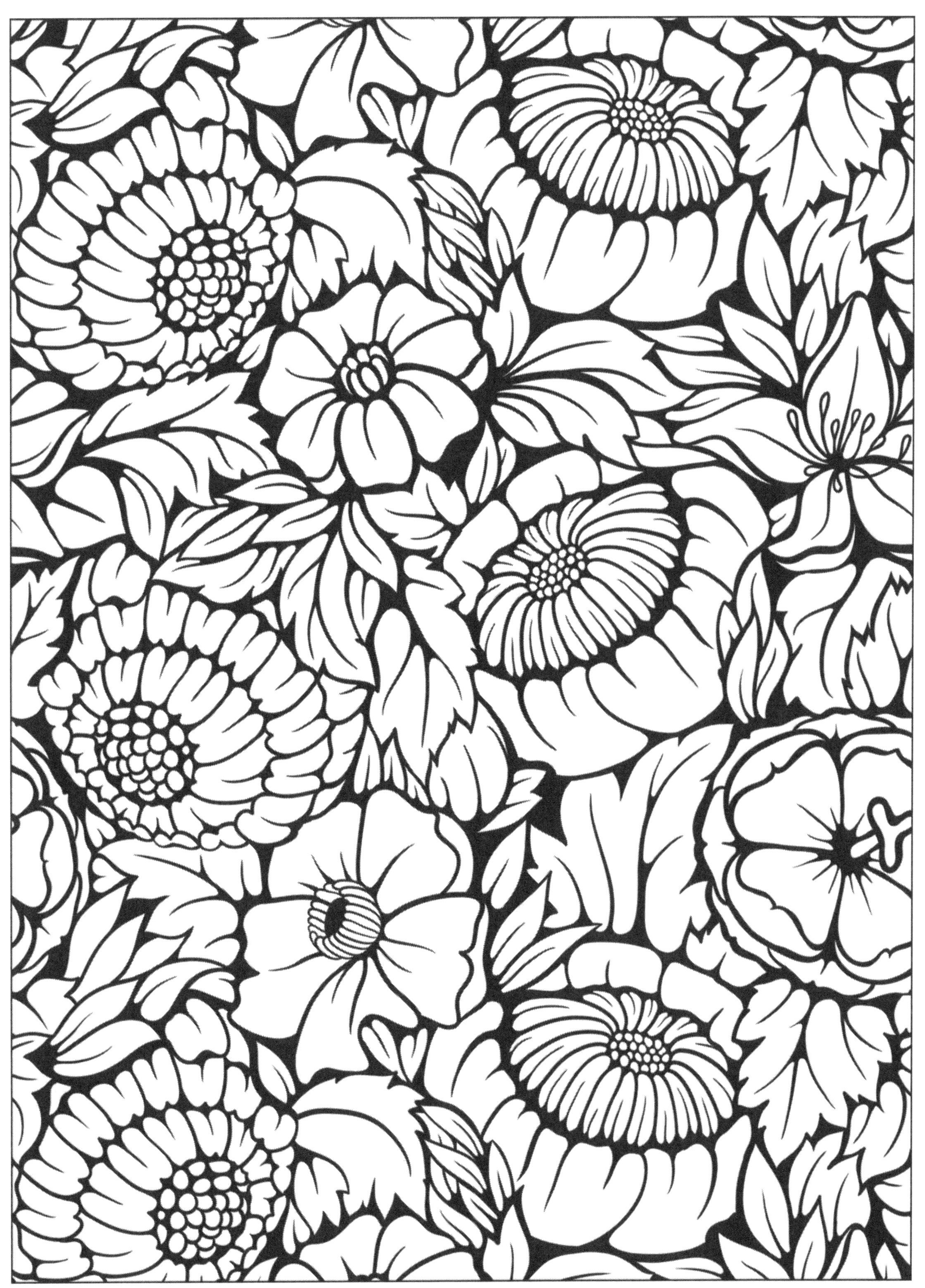

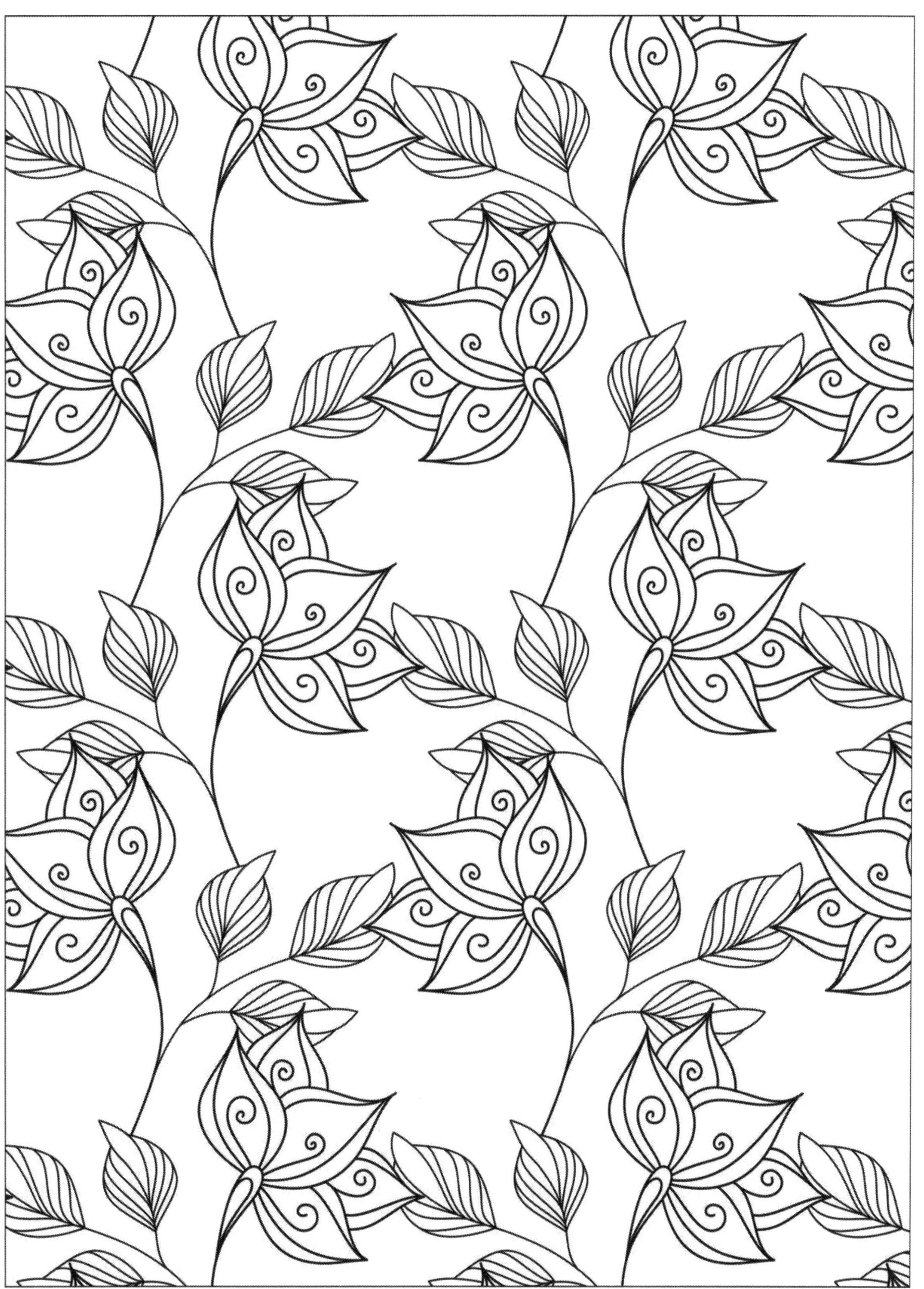

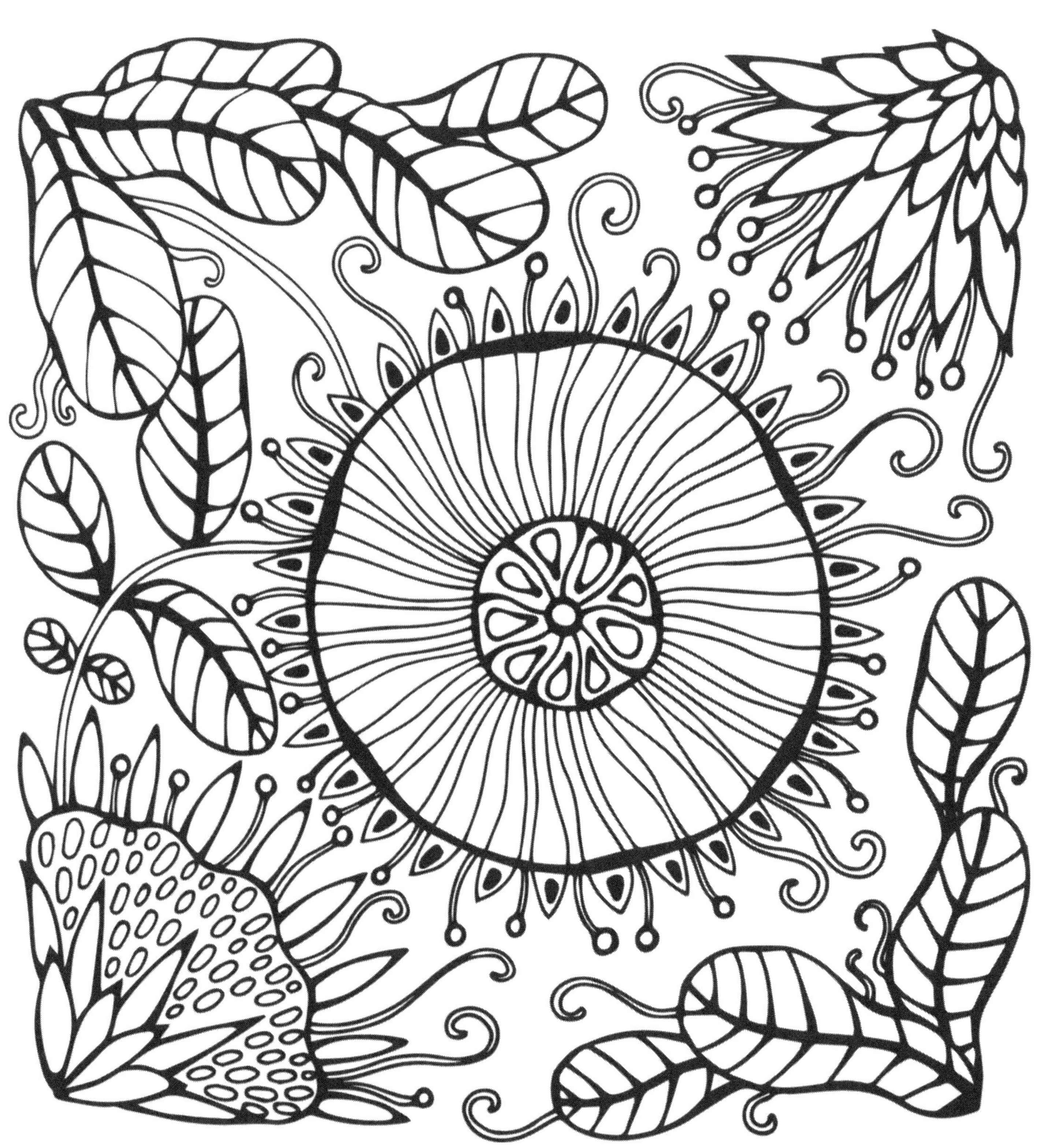

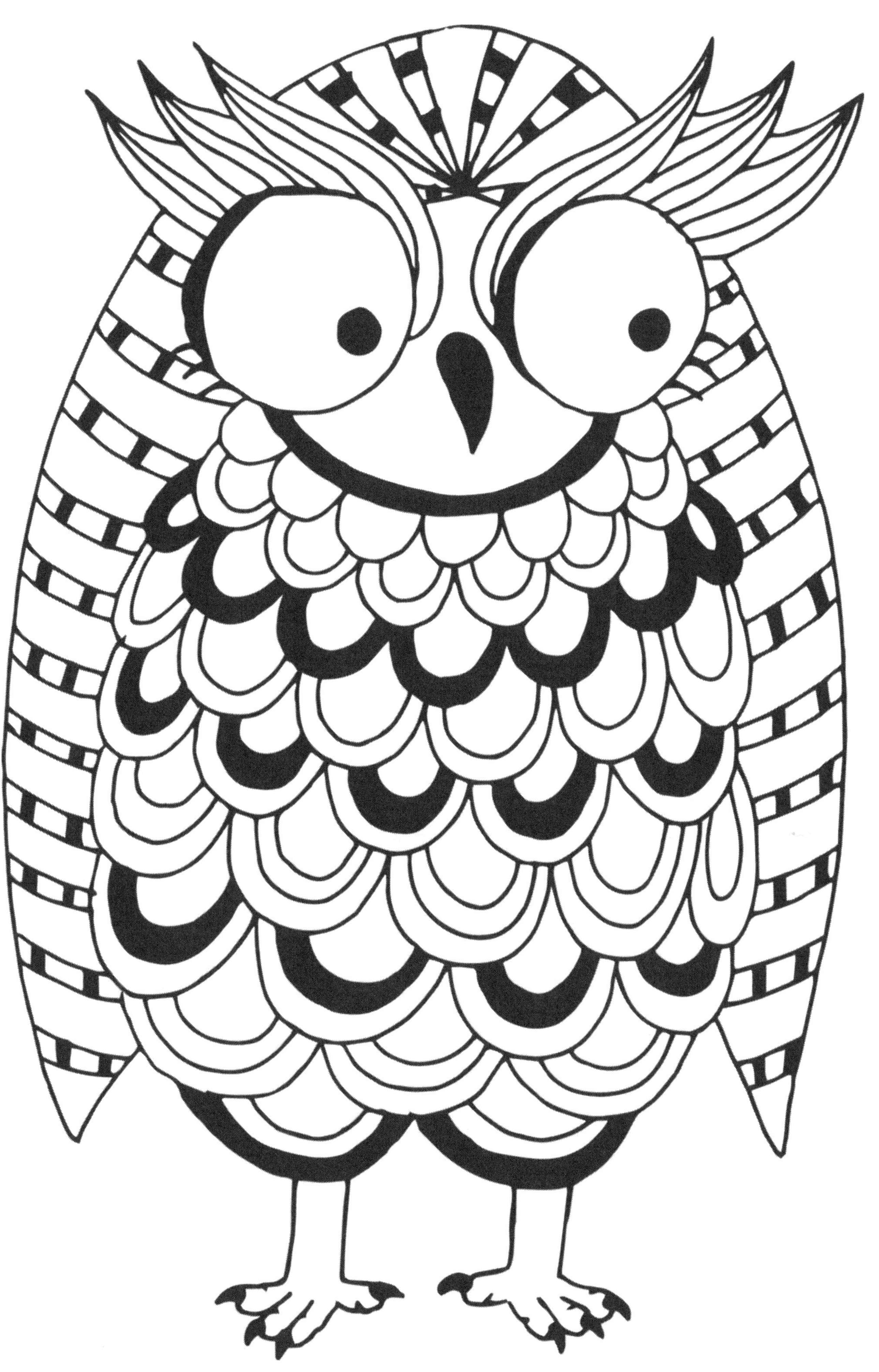

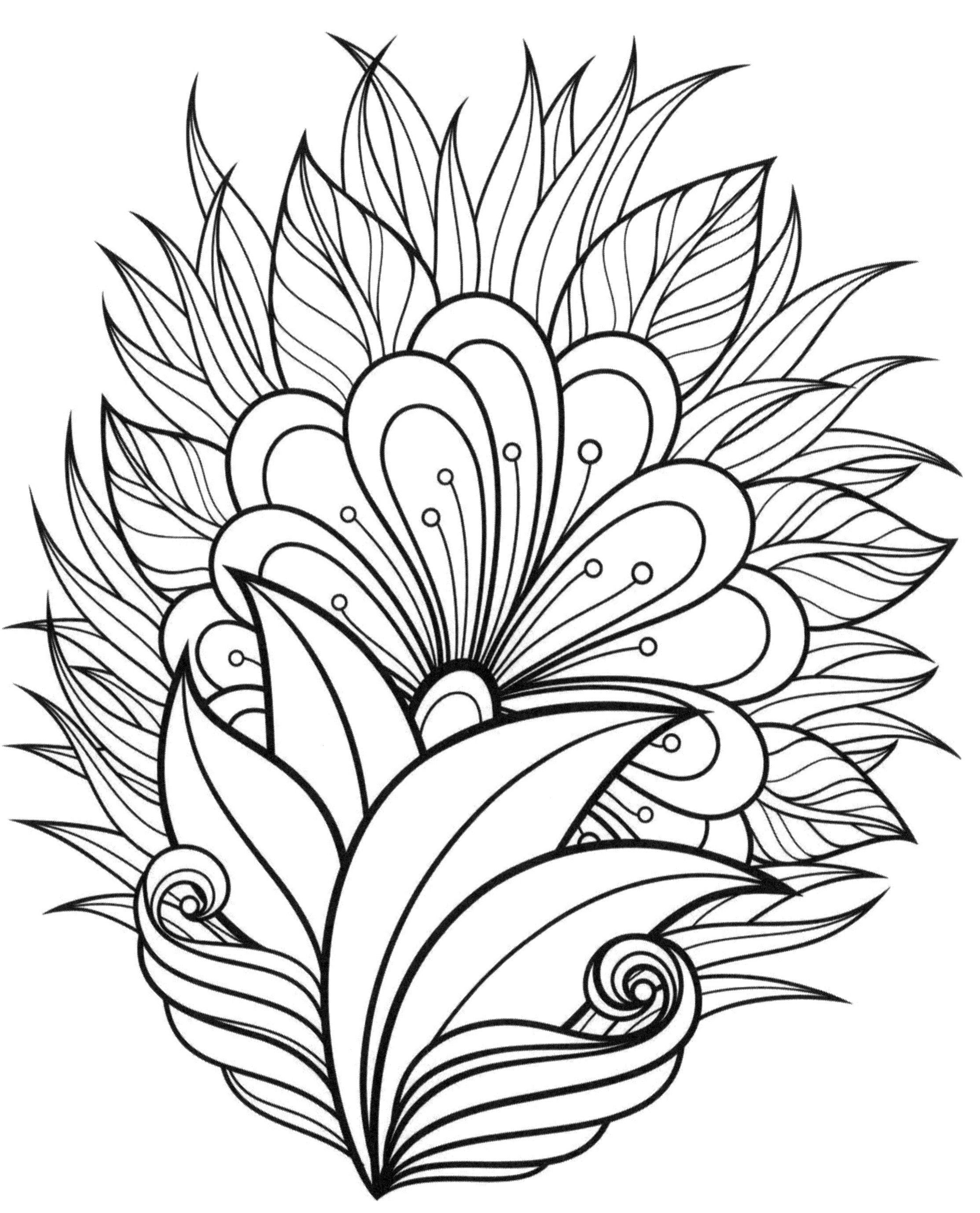

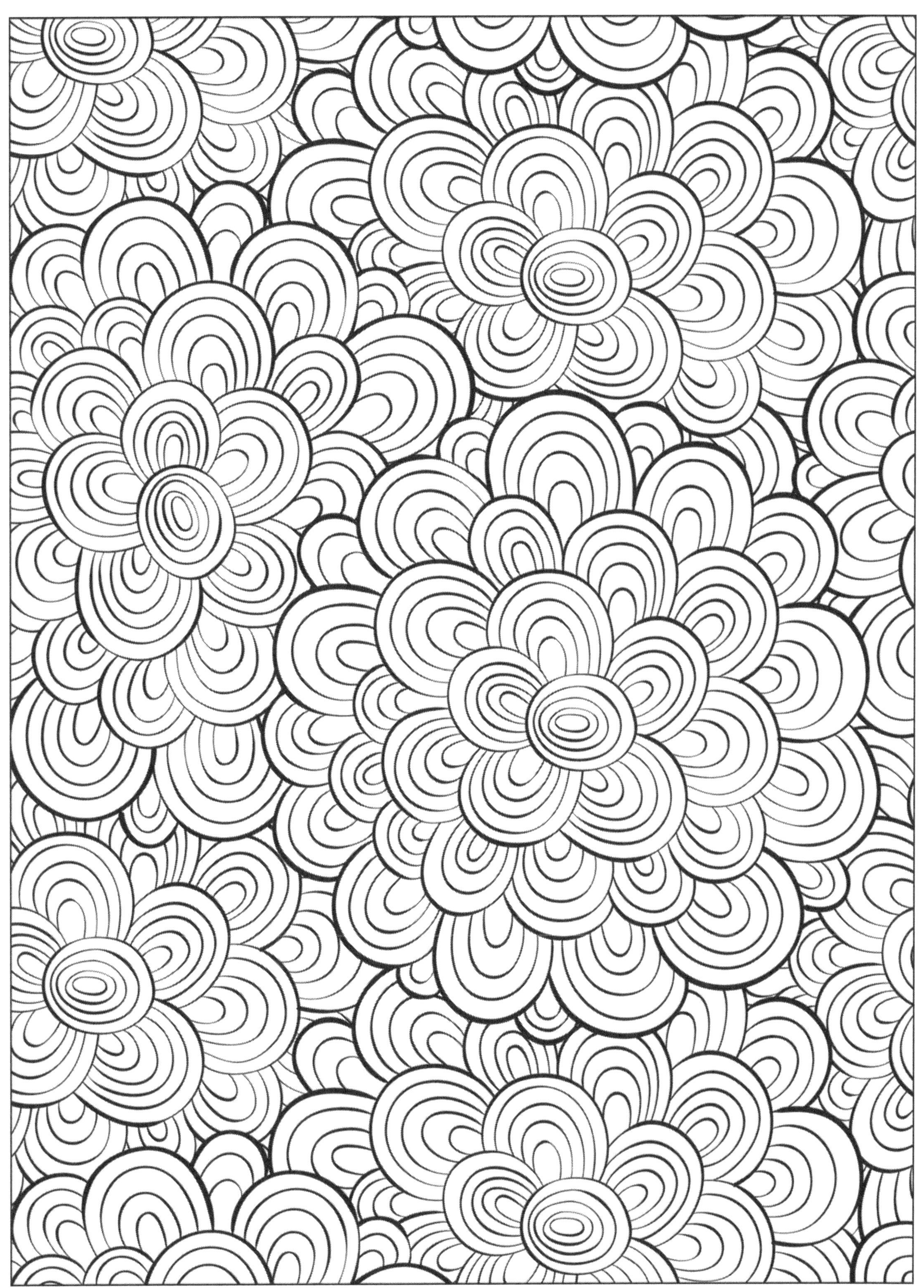

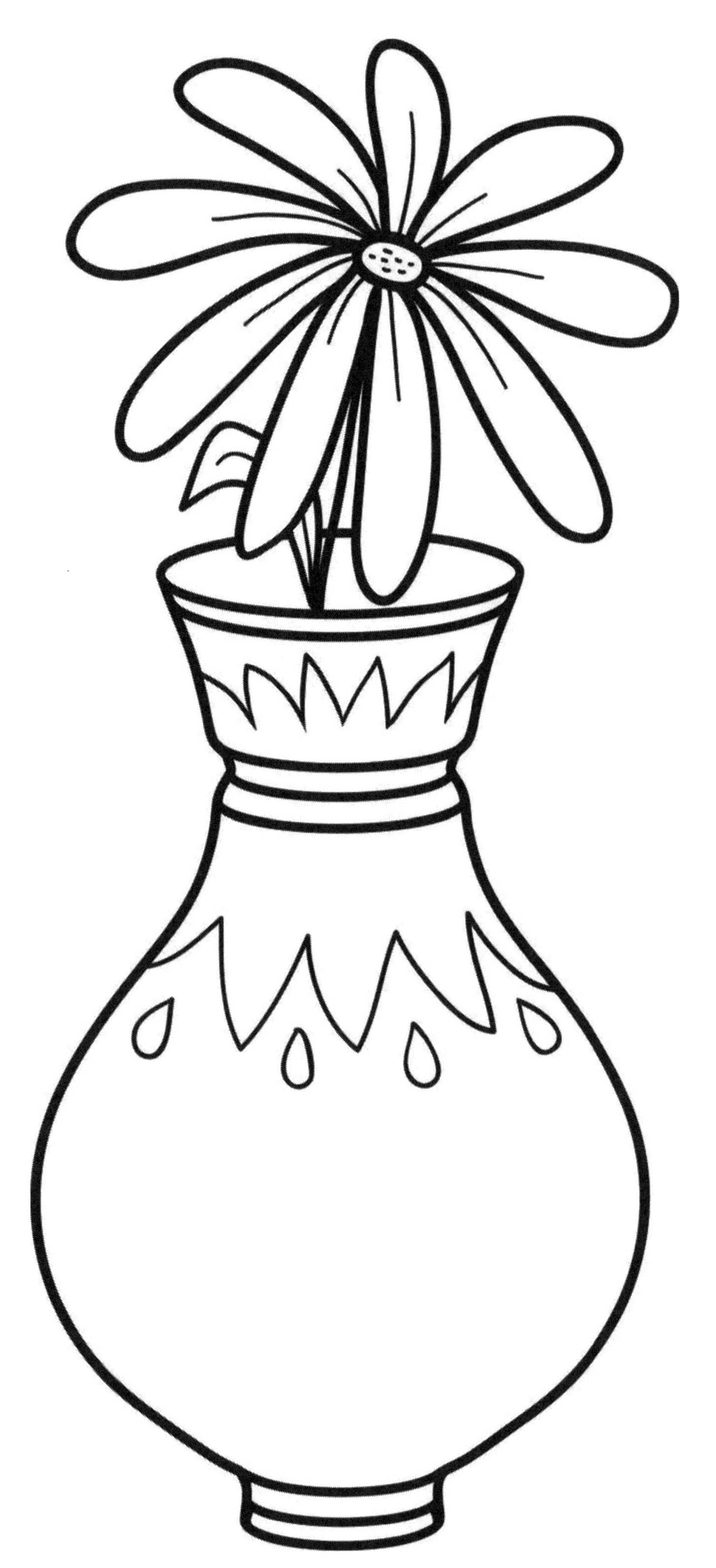

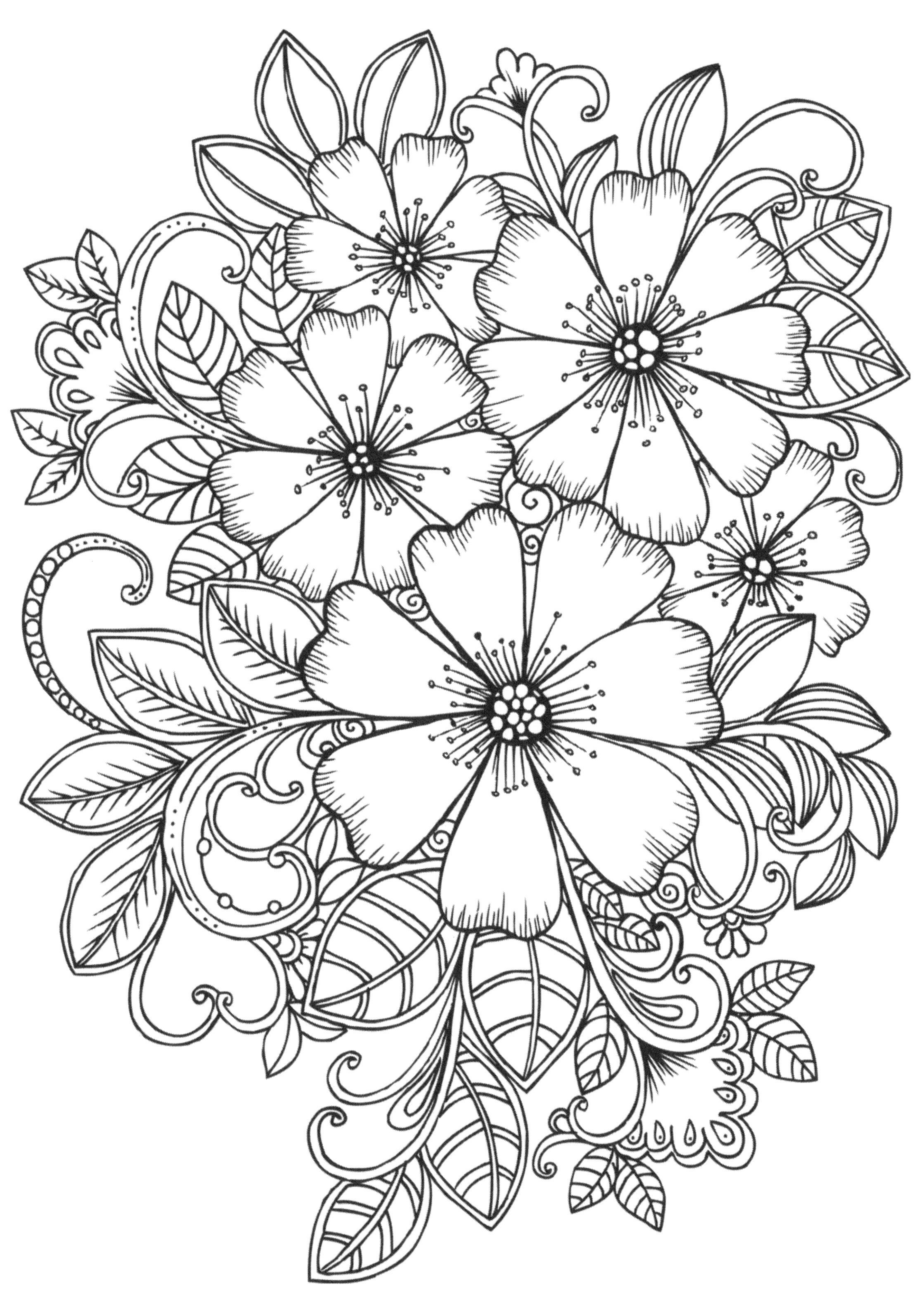

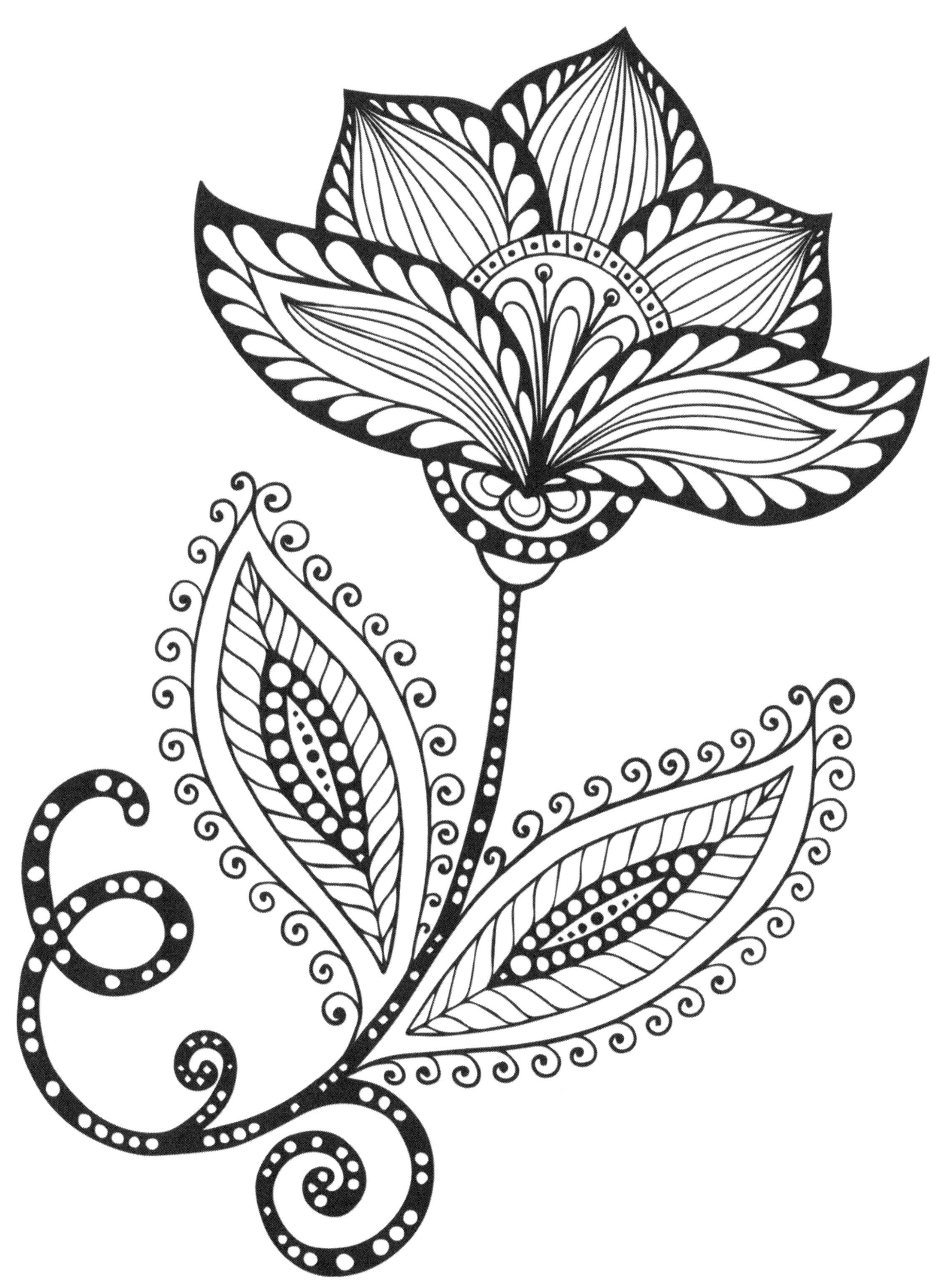

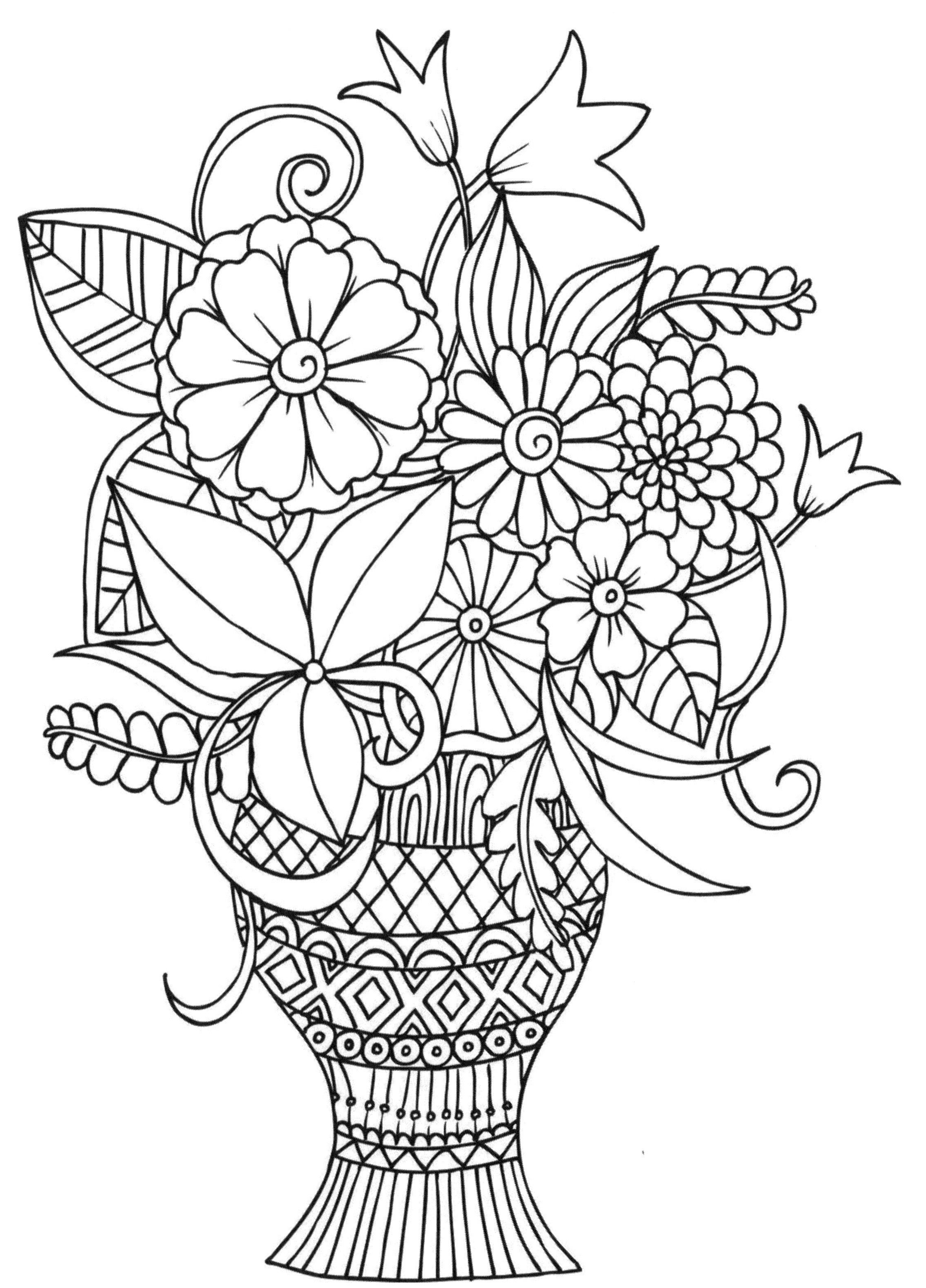

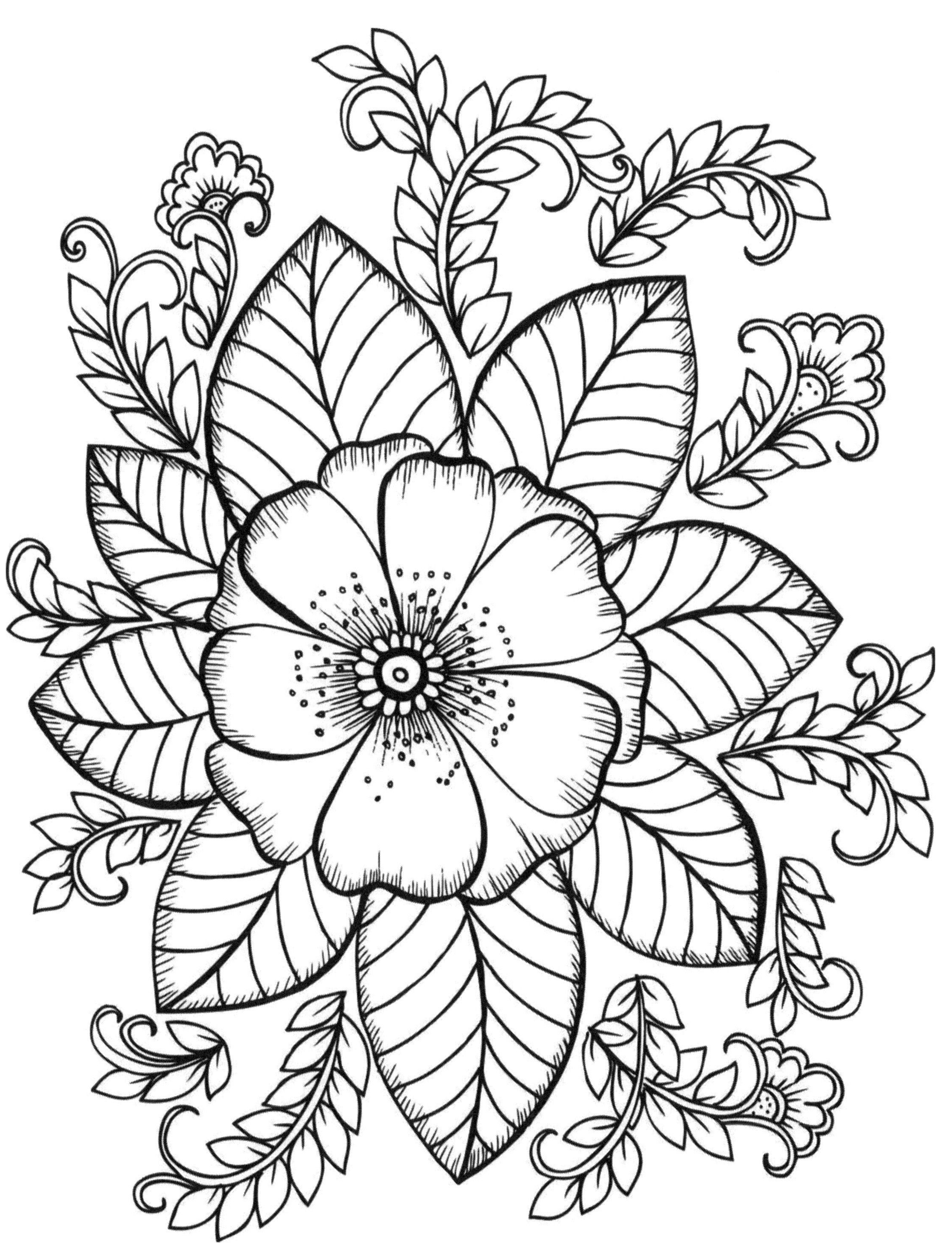

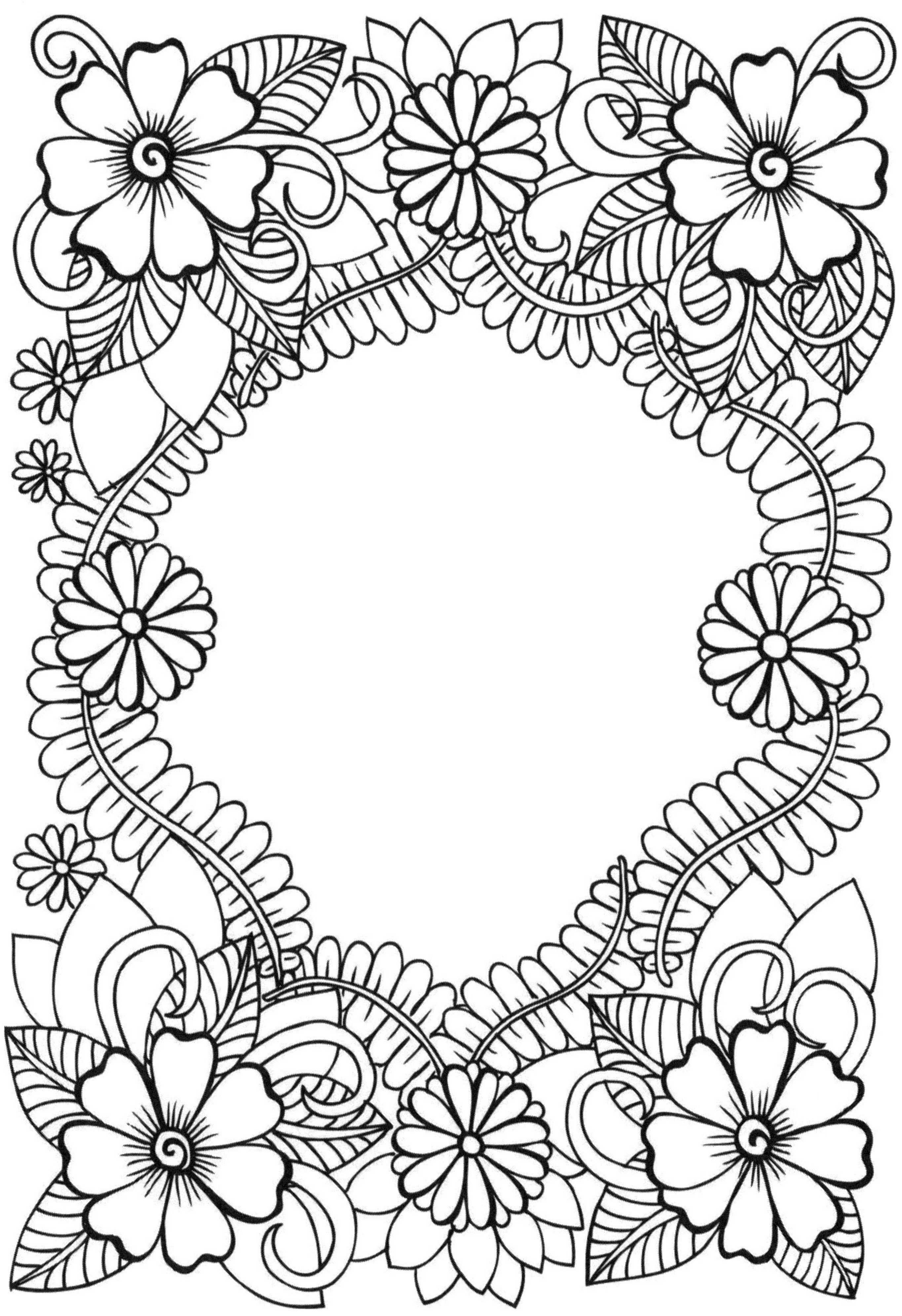

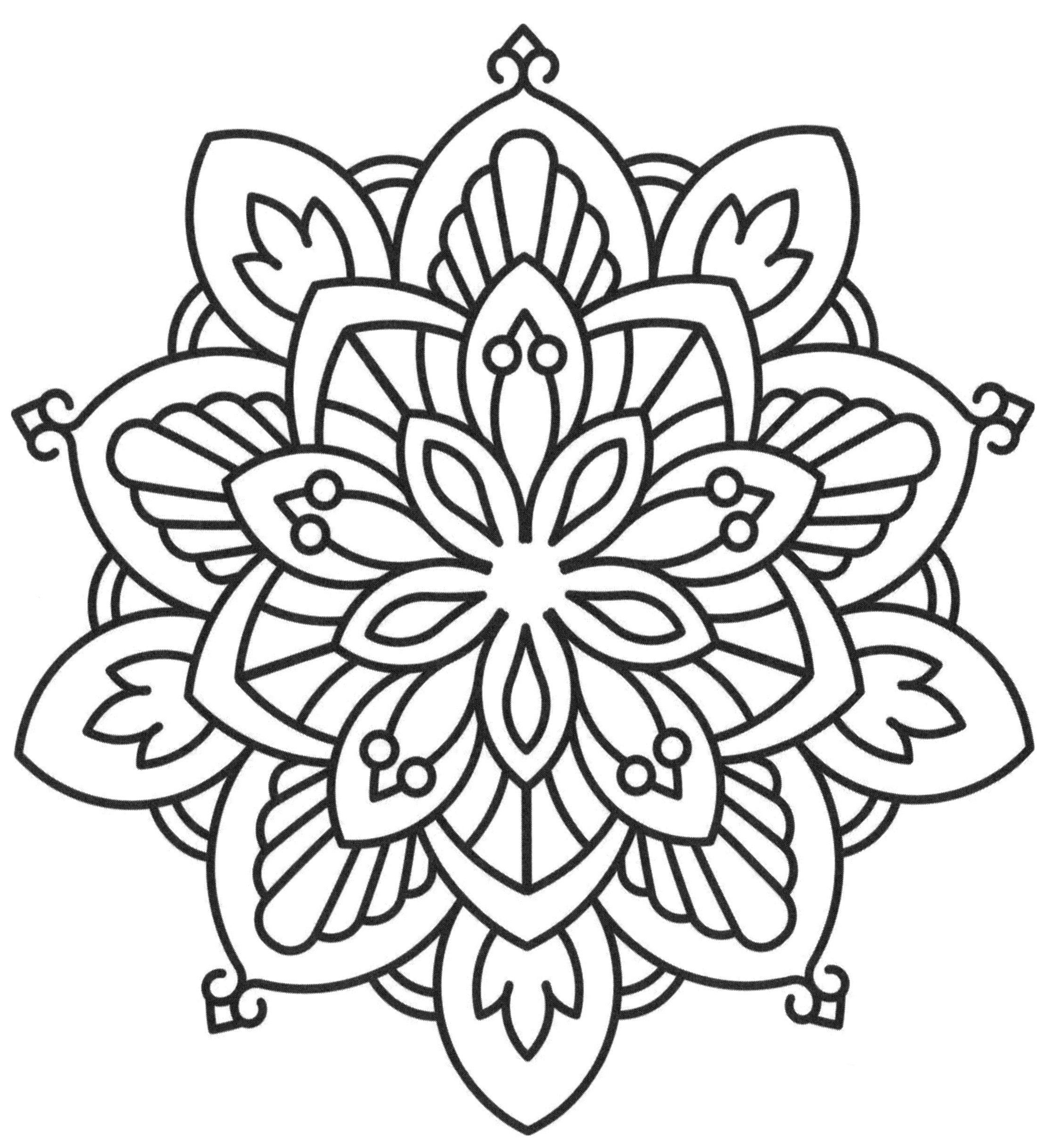

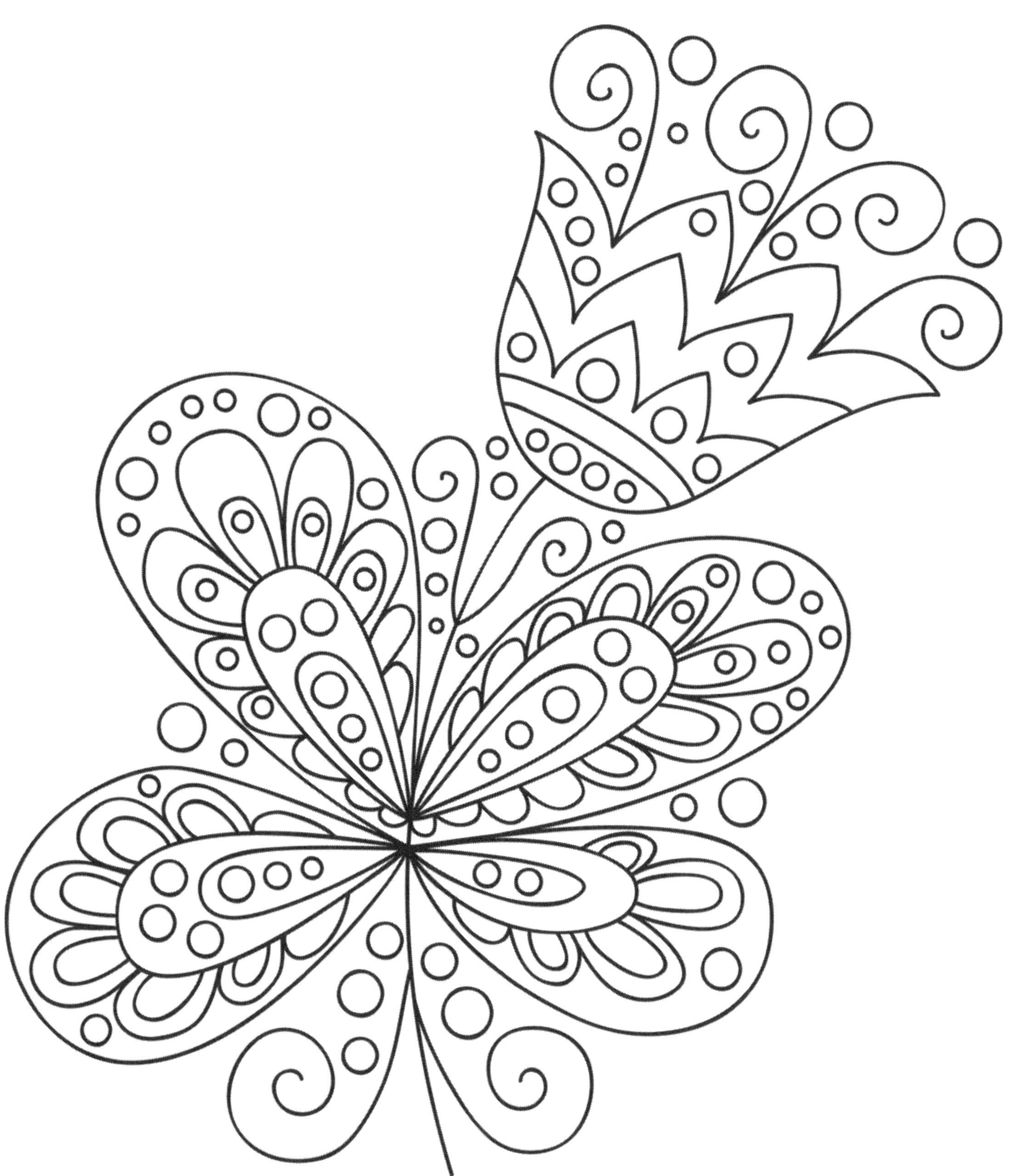

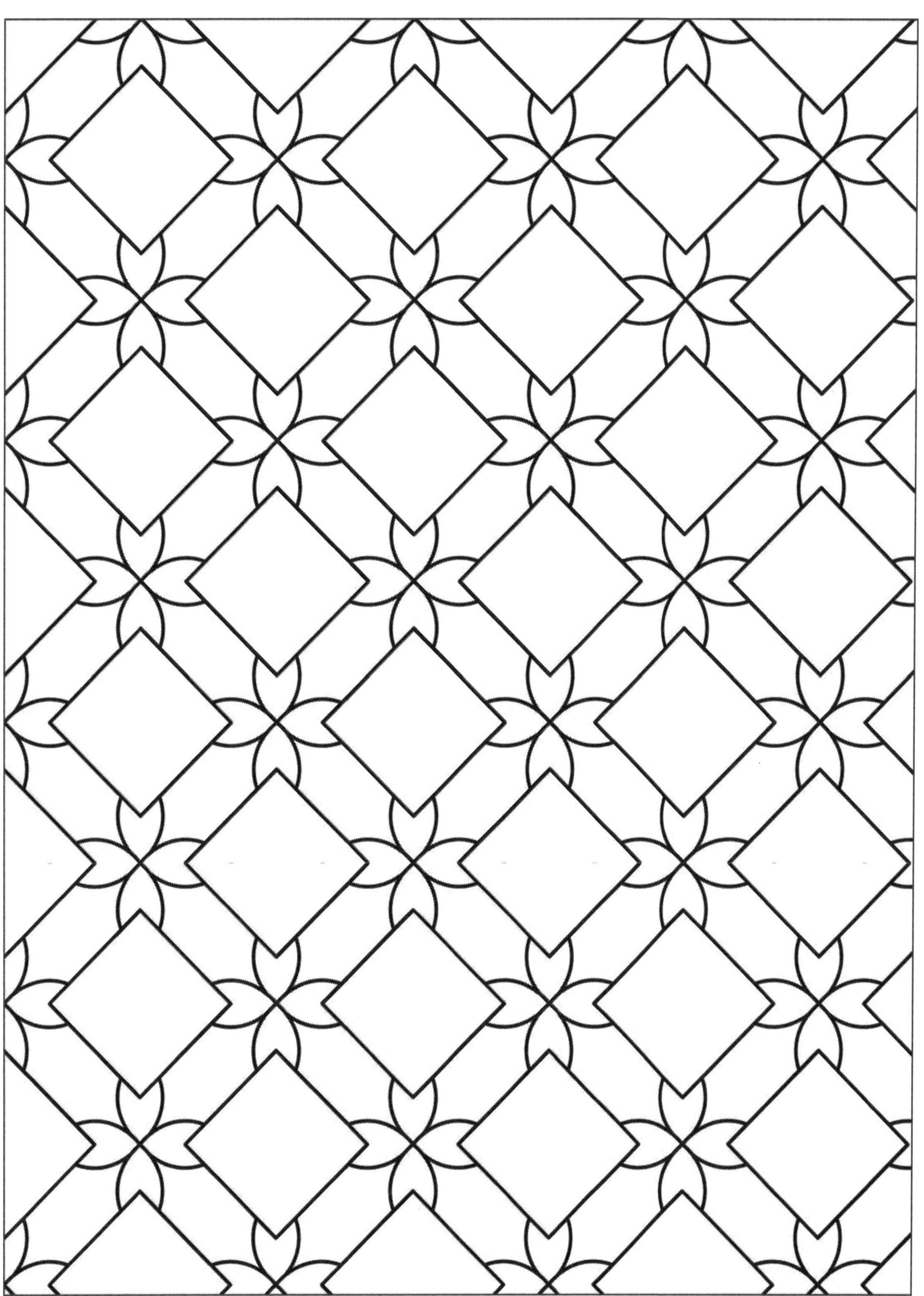

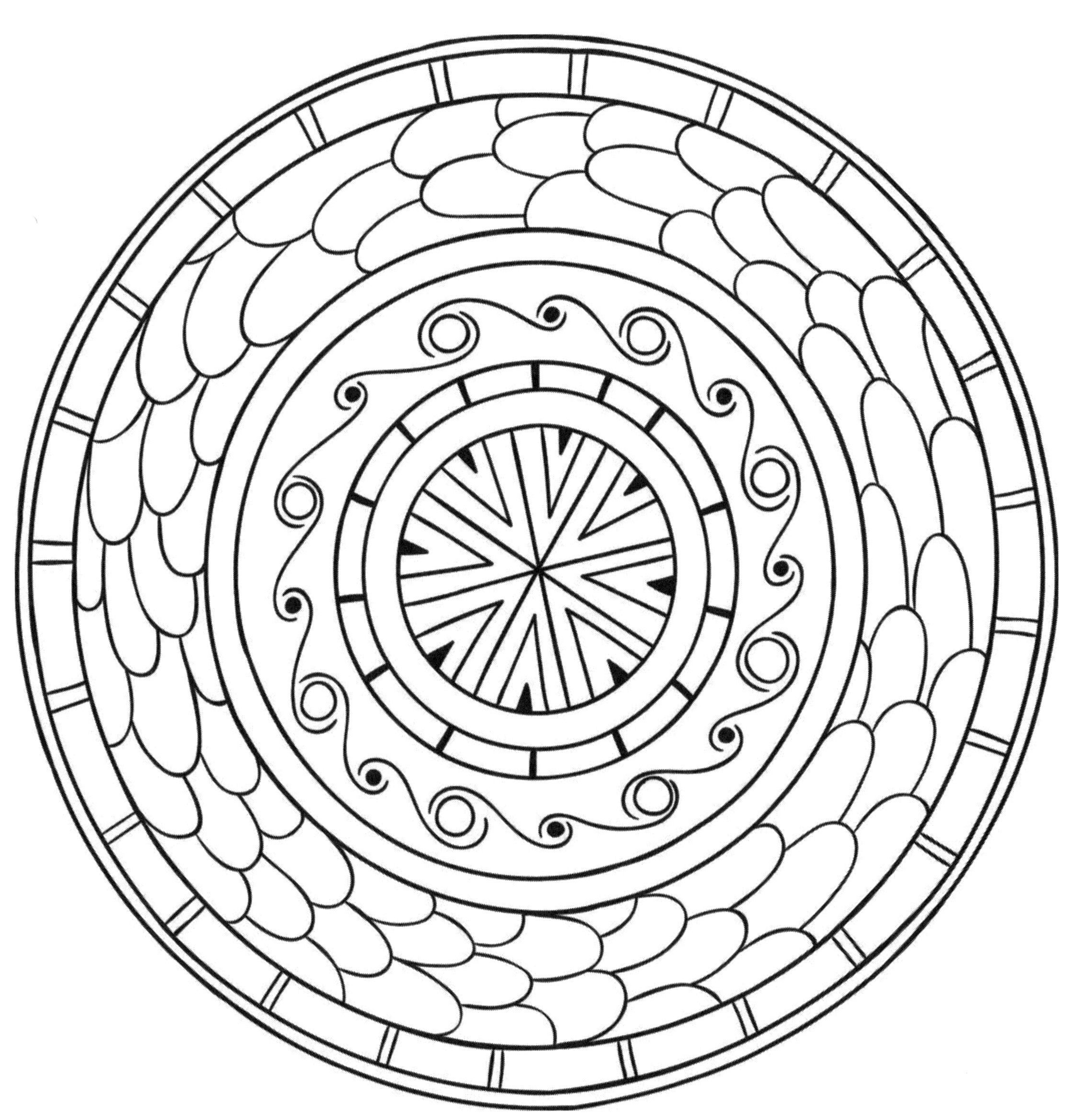

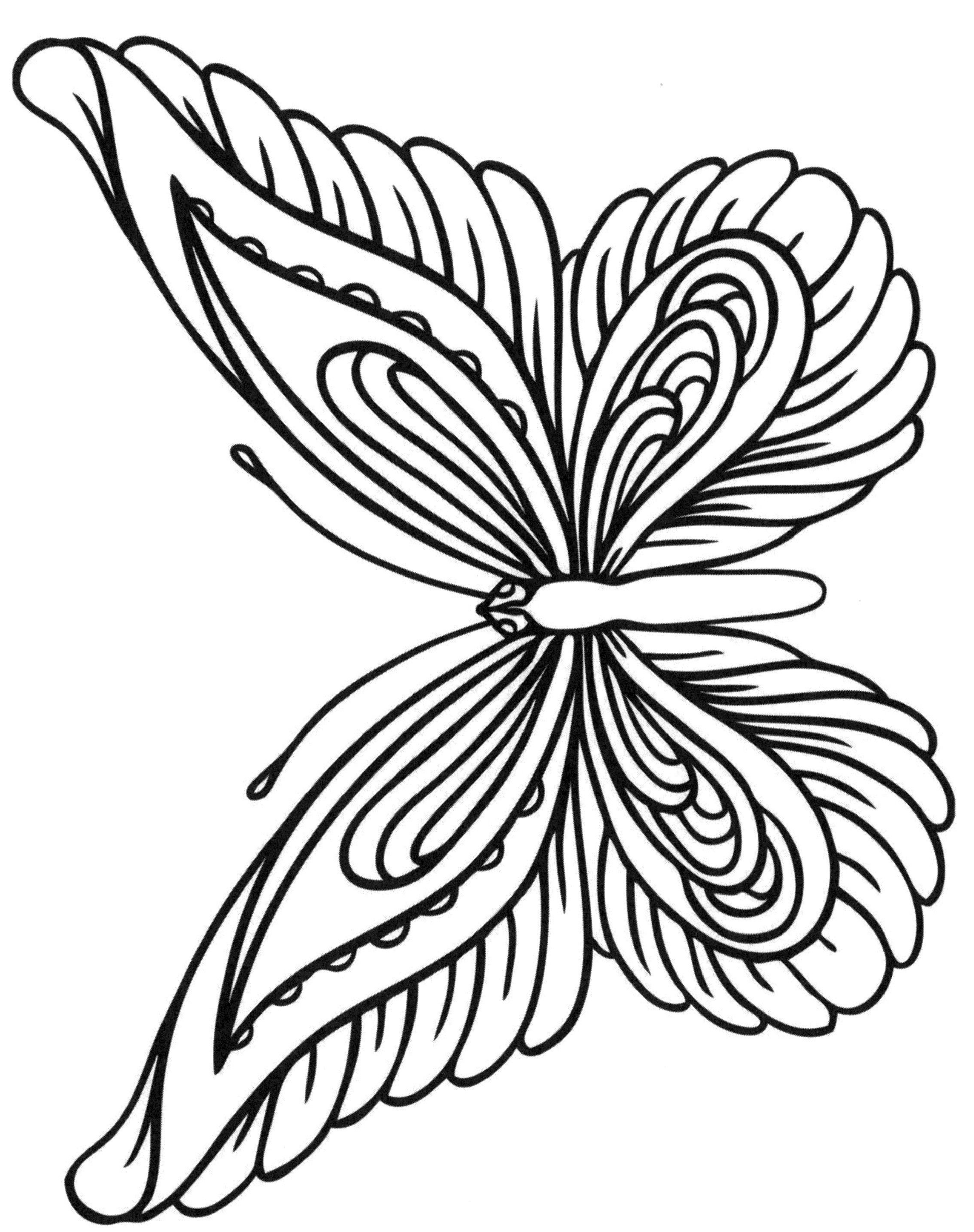

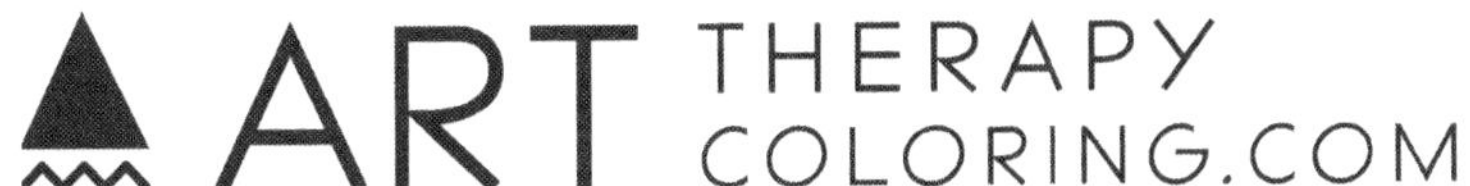

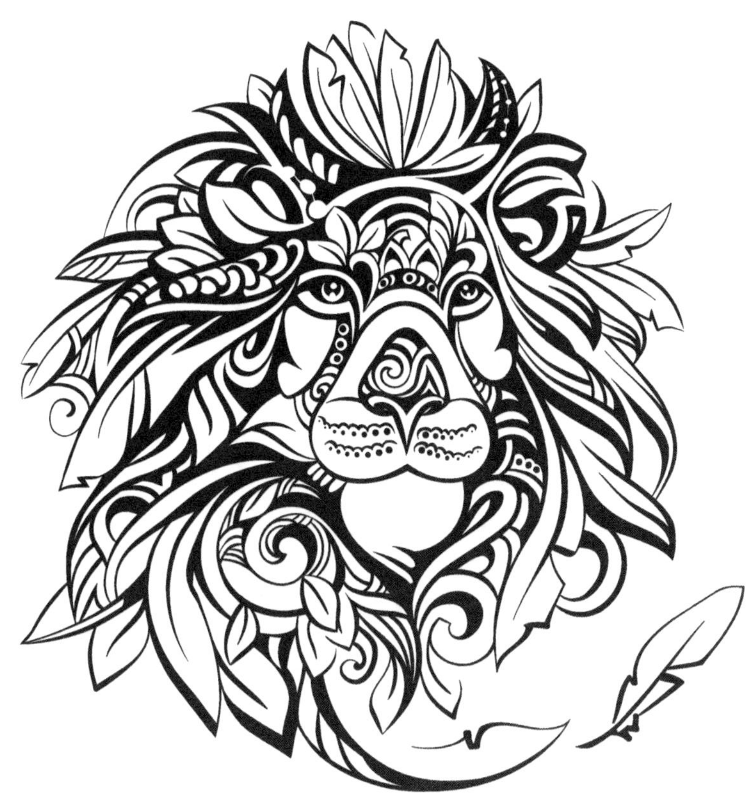

Did You Enjoy Our Coloring Book?

We Want To Hear About It!

Help spread the word about our coloring books! The best way to spread the word is through reviews. We know how busy you are, especially with all of that coloring, but we would appreciate it!

Visit our website at www.arttherapycoloring.com

Over 200 Art Therapy Coloring Books

See our collection of over 200 Art Therapy Coloring Books for Adults, Men, Women, Seniors, Teens, Kids, Boys, and Girls.

Coloring Books For Seniors

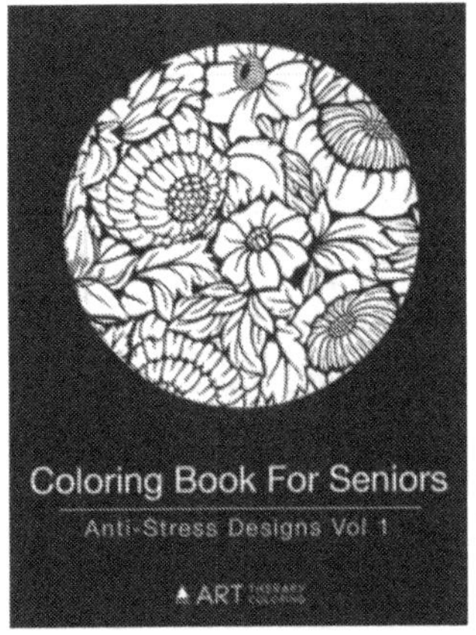

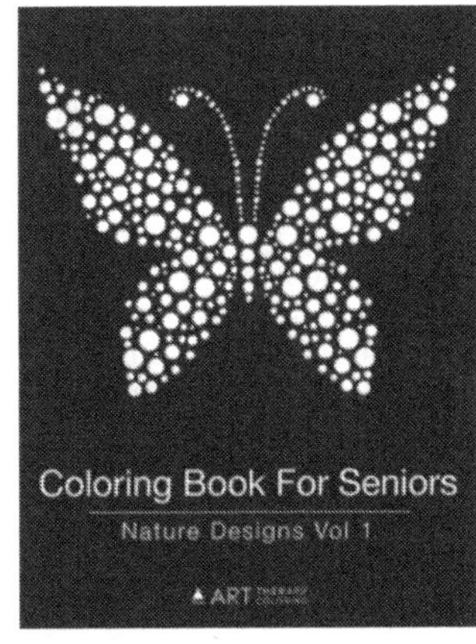

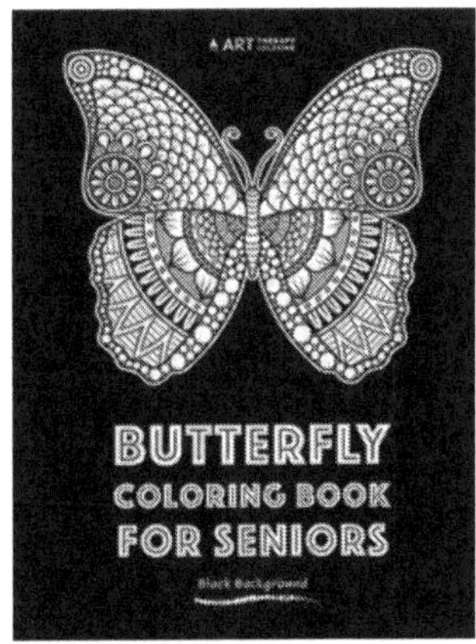

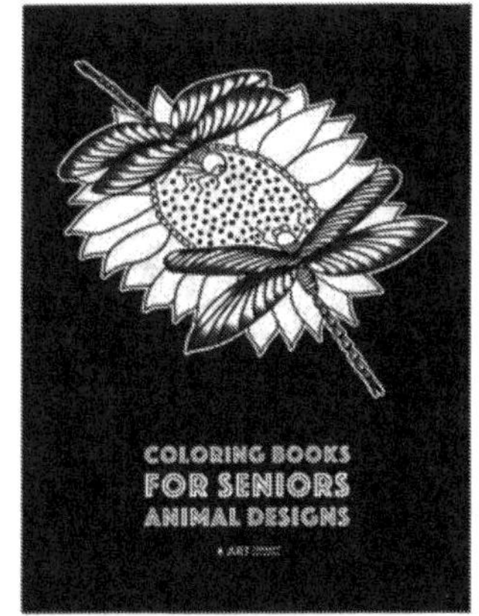

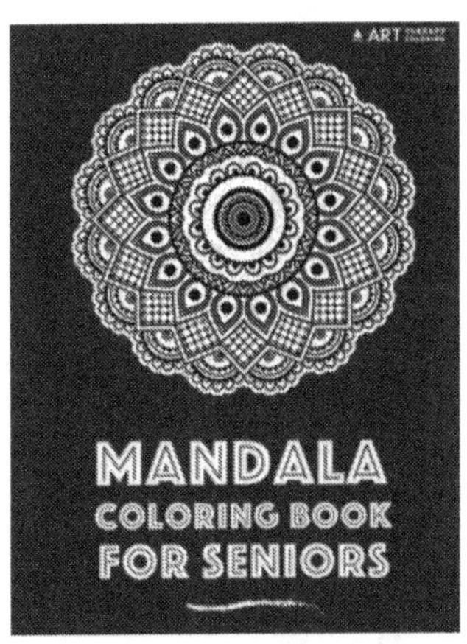

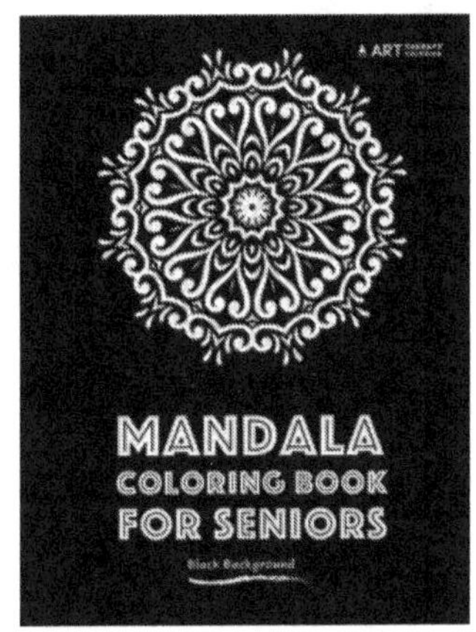

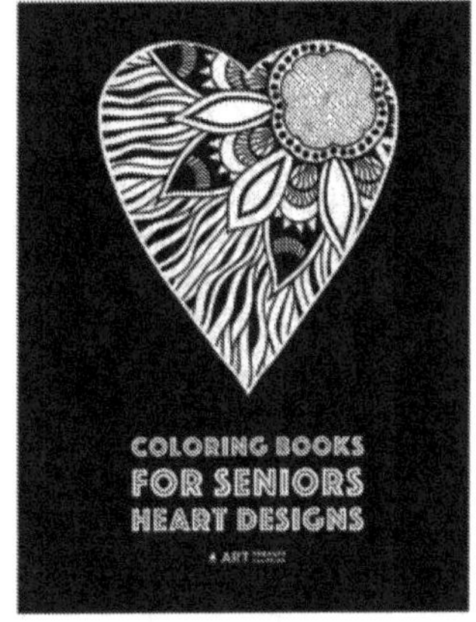

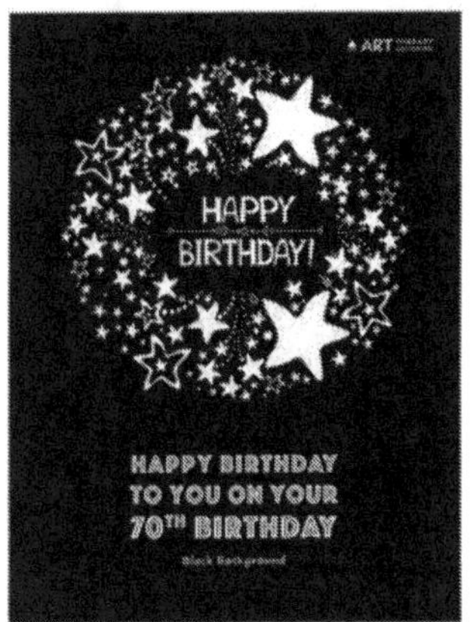

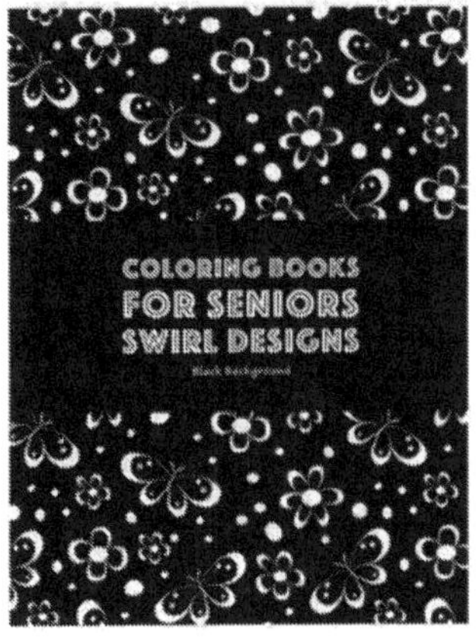

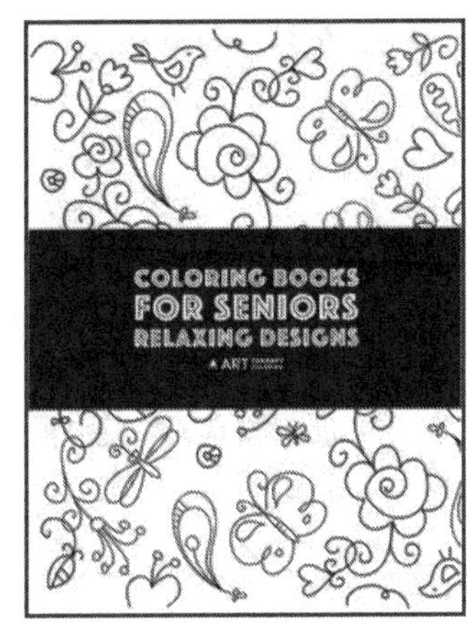

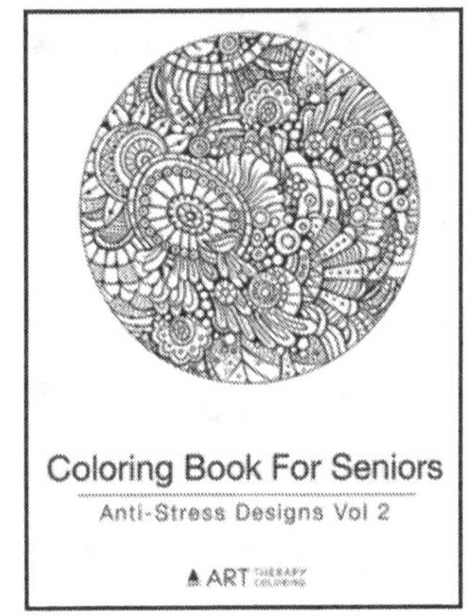

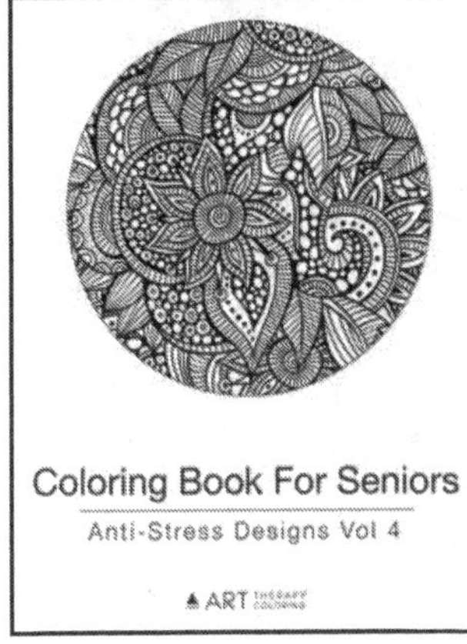

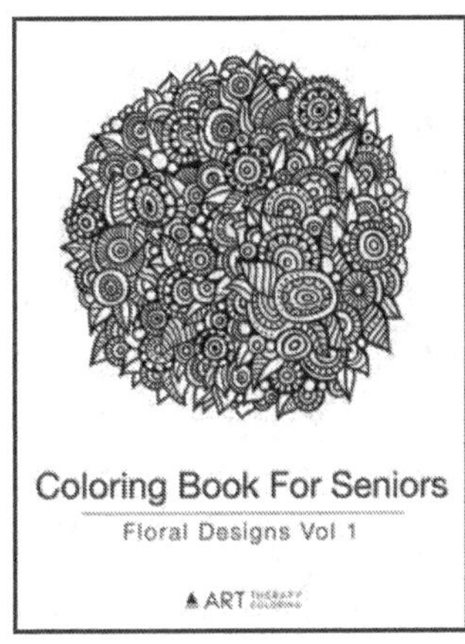

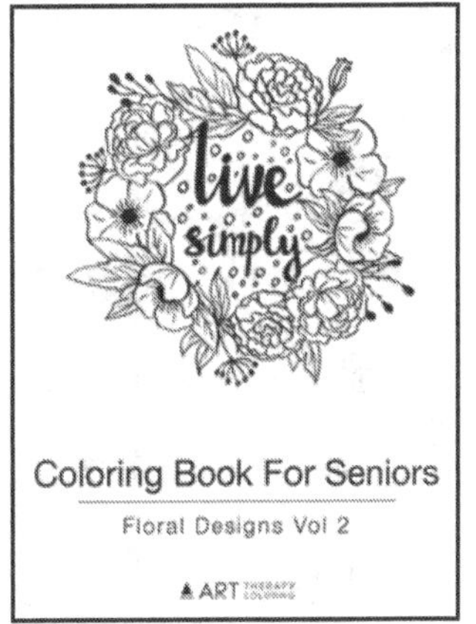

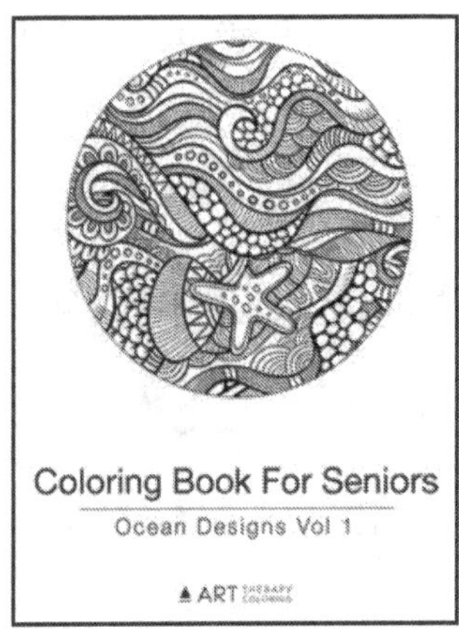

Coloring Books For Adults

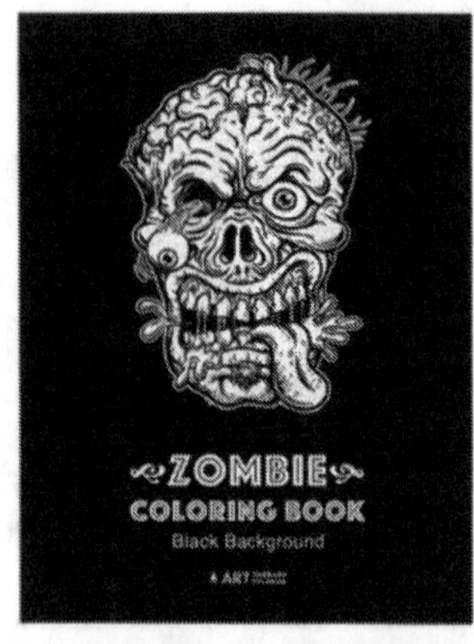

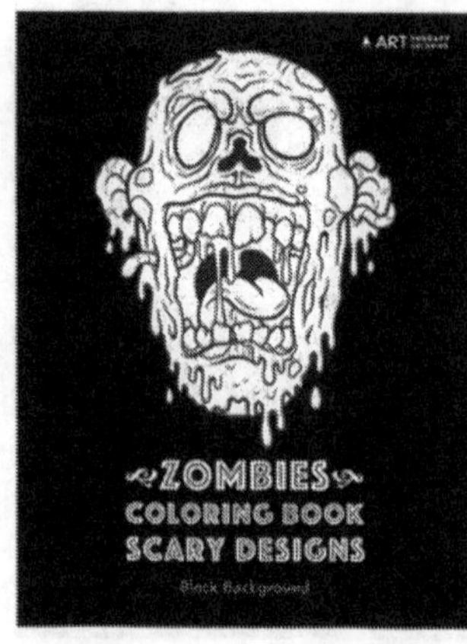

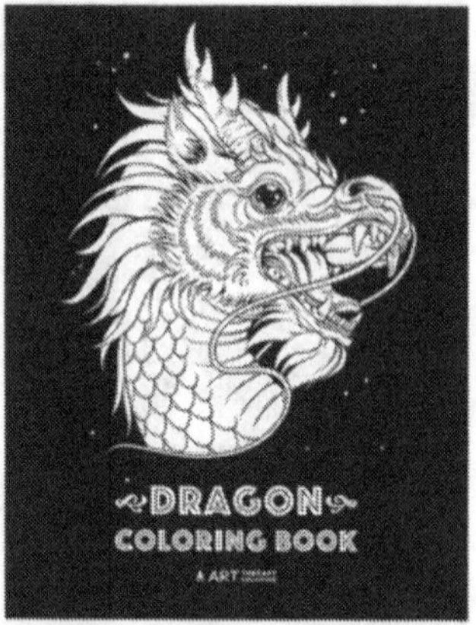

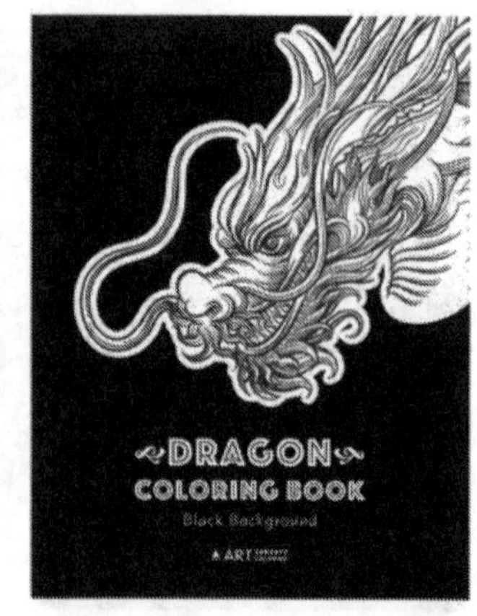

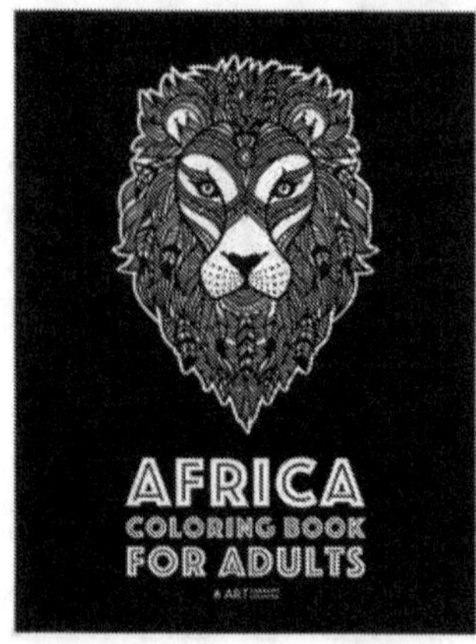

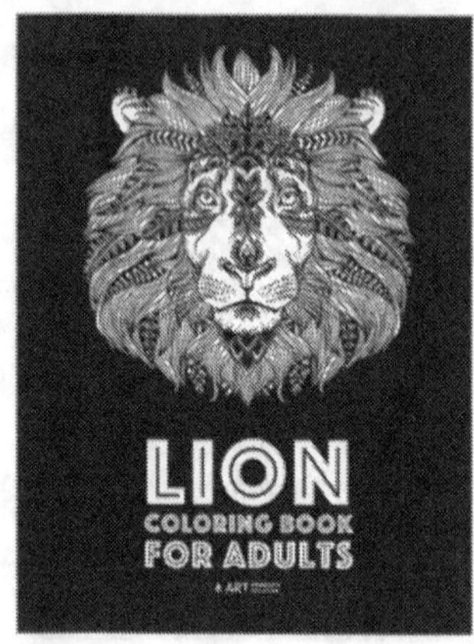

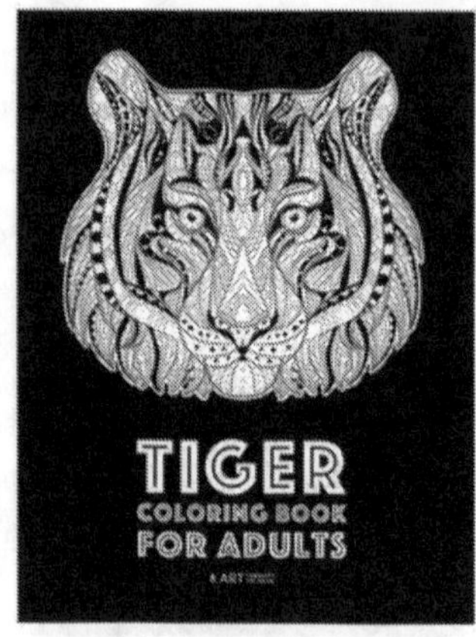

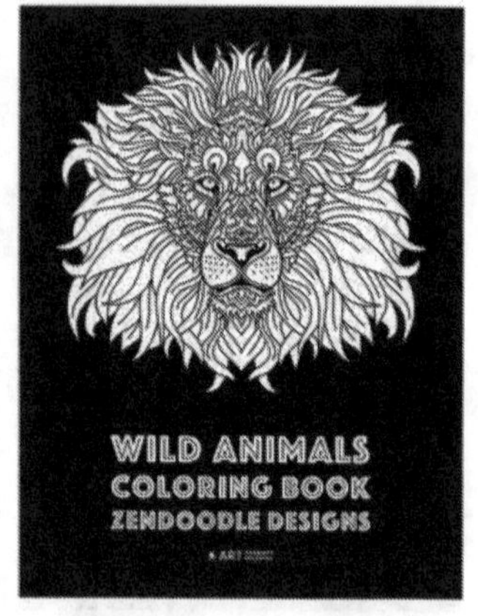

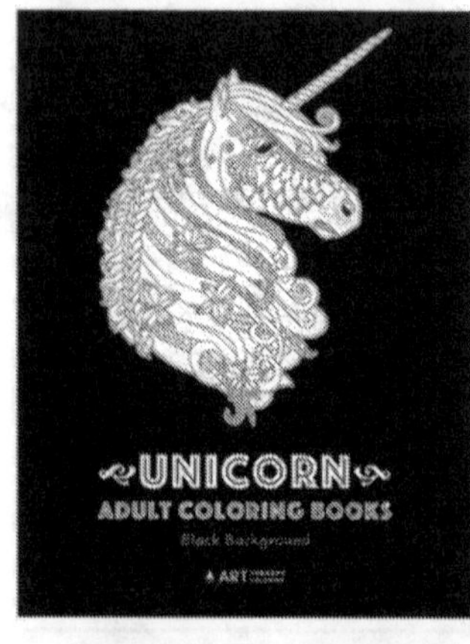

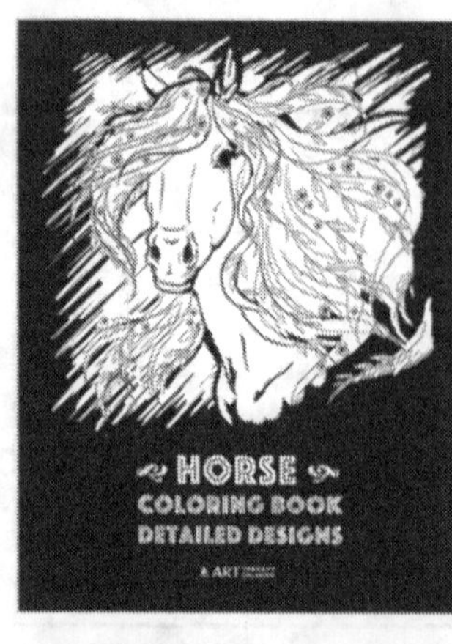

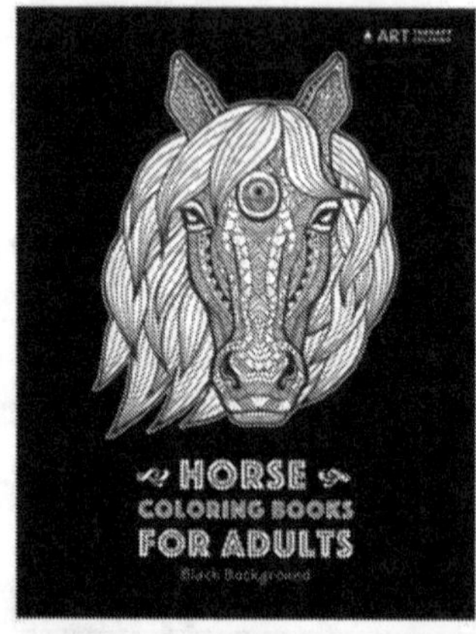

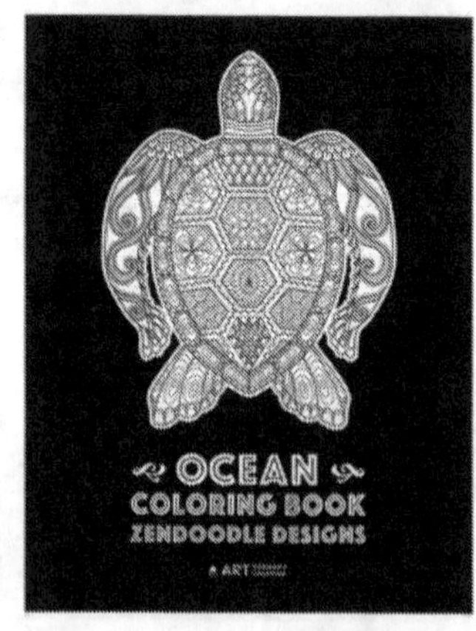

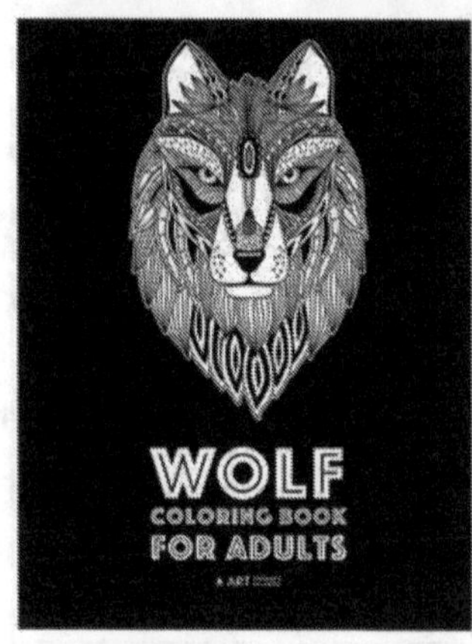

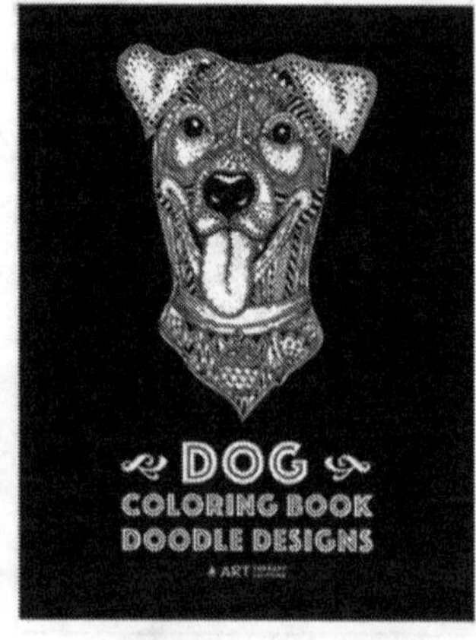

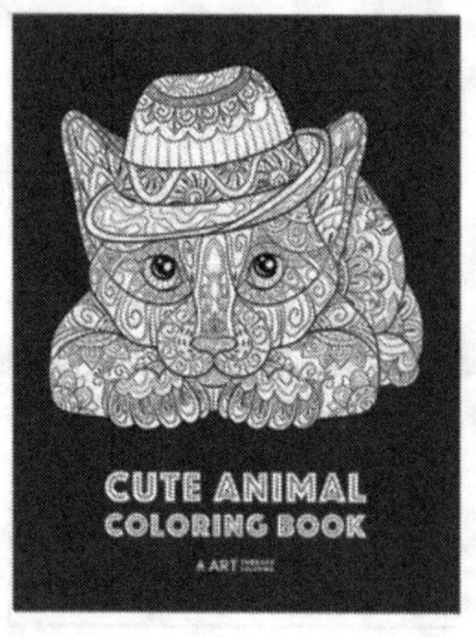

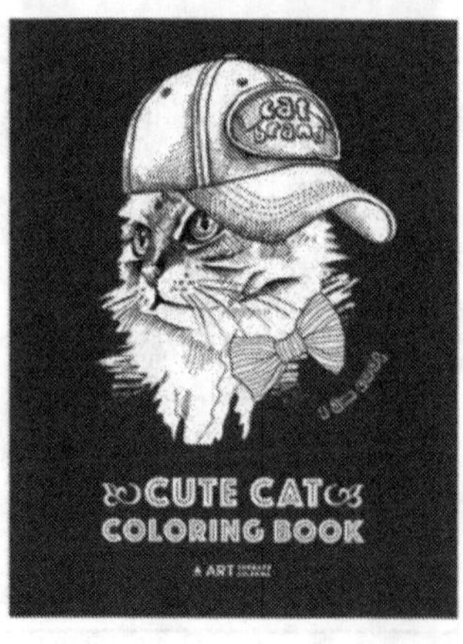

Coloring Books For Adults

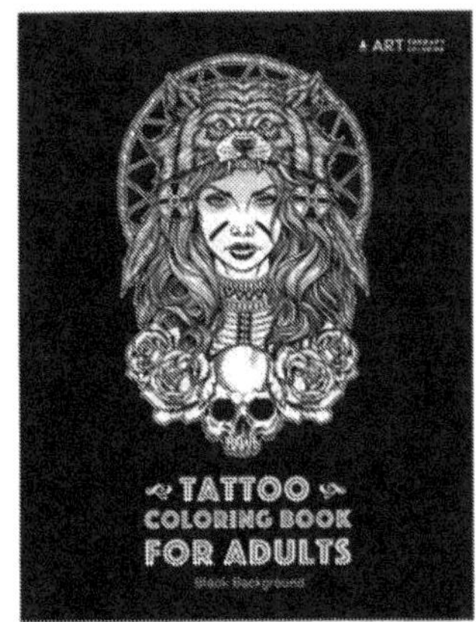

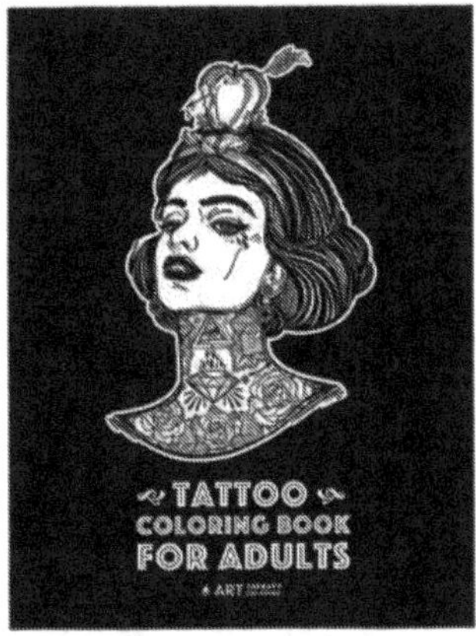

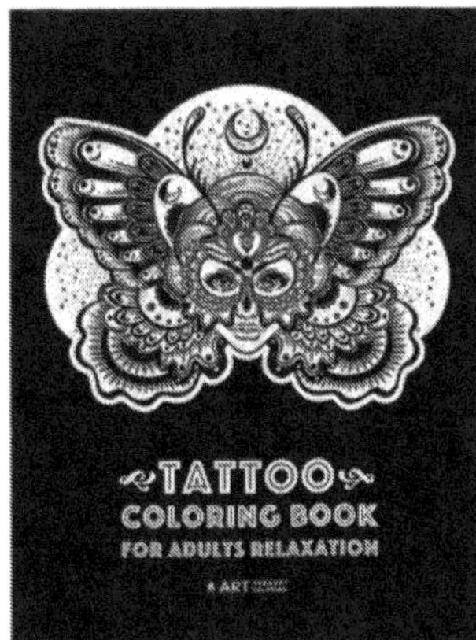

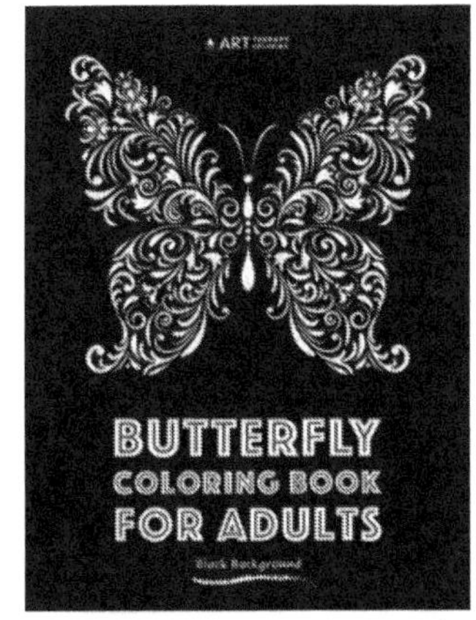

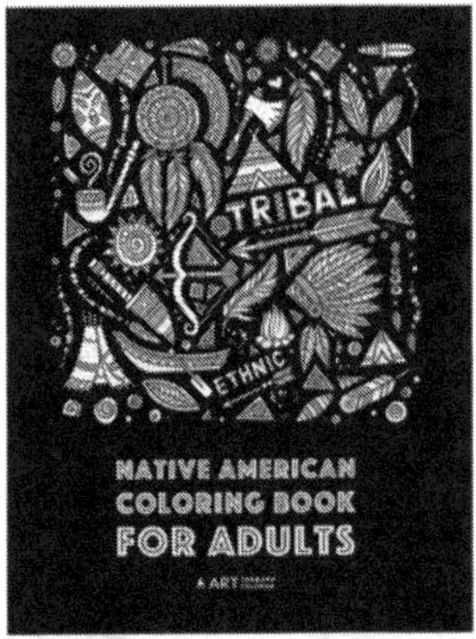

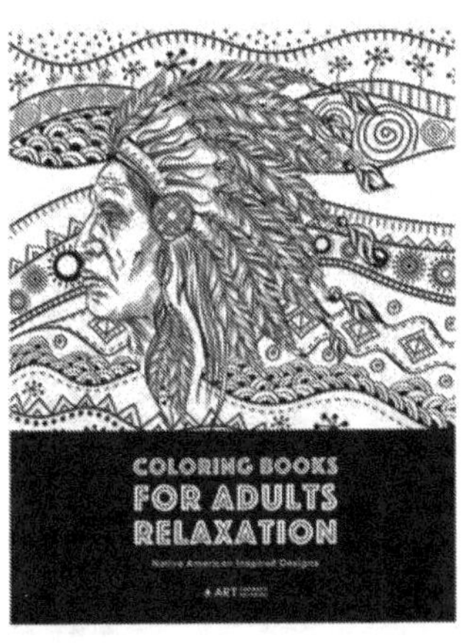

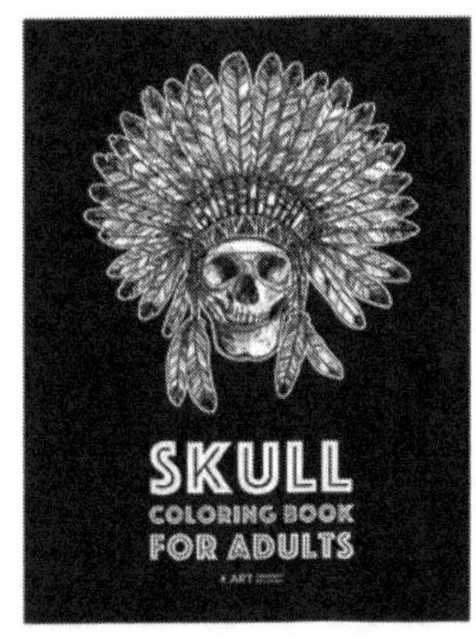

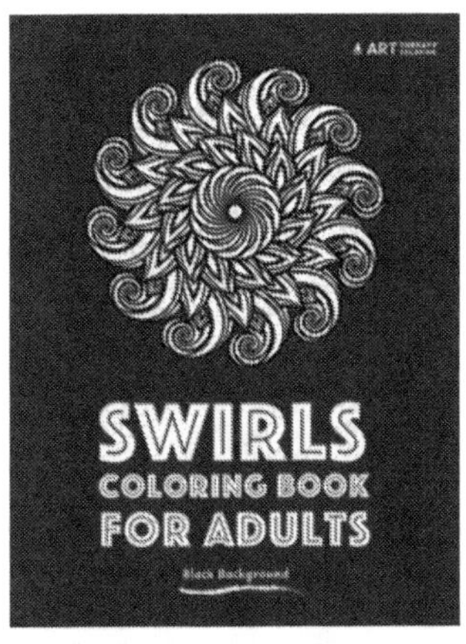

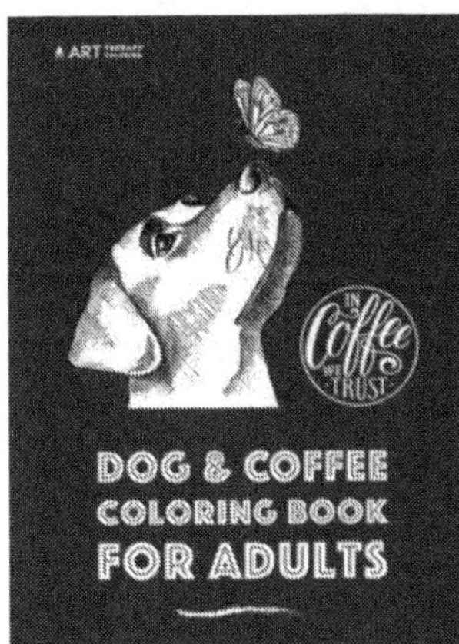

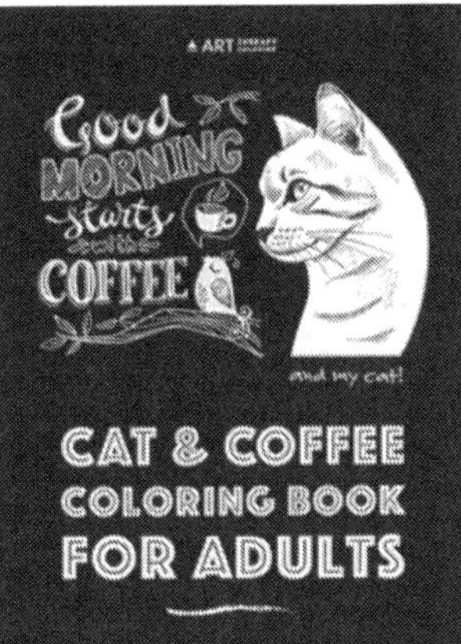

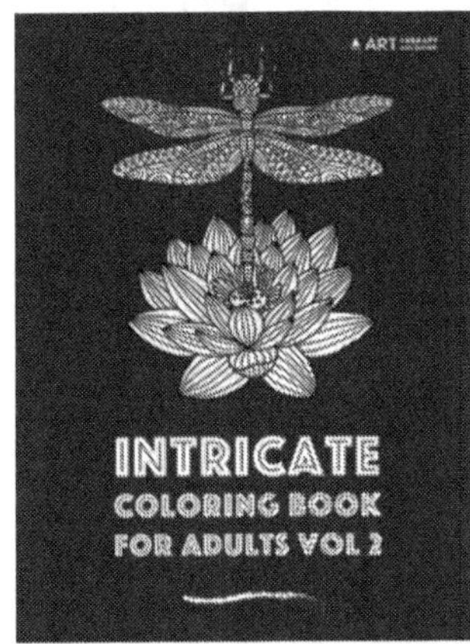

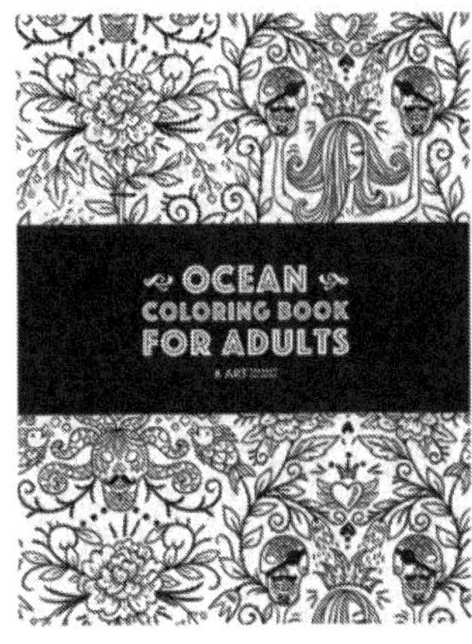

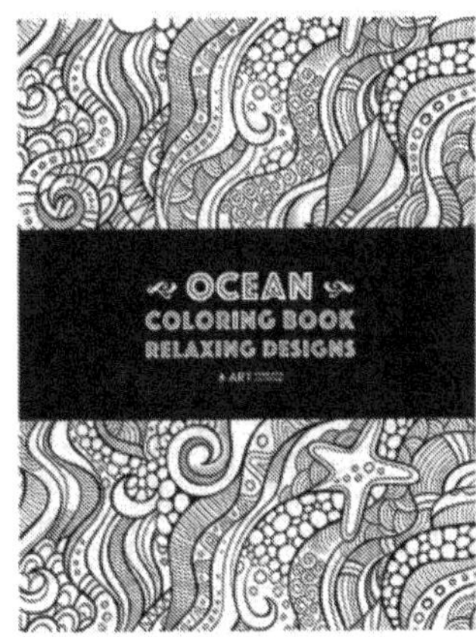

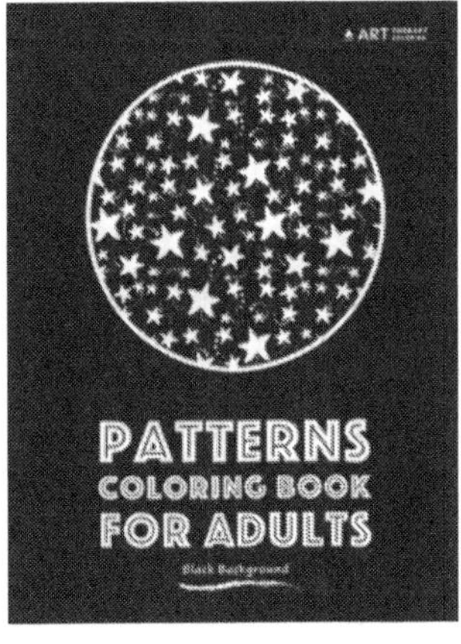

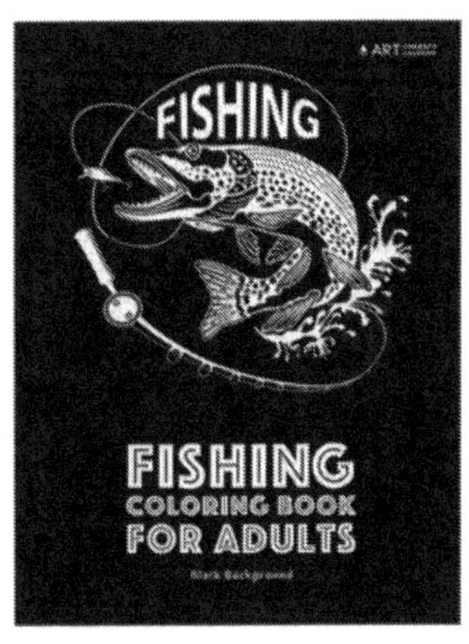

Coloring Books For Adults

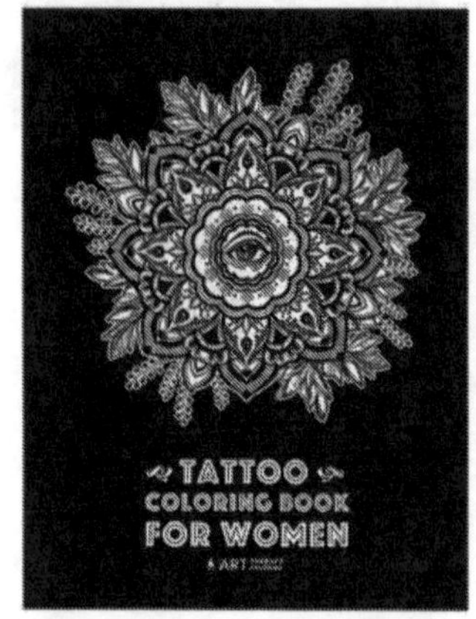

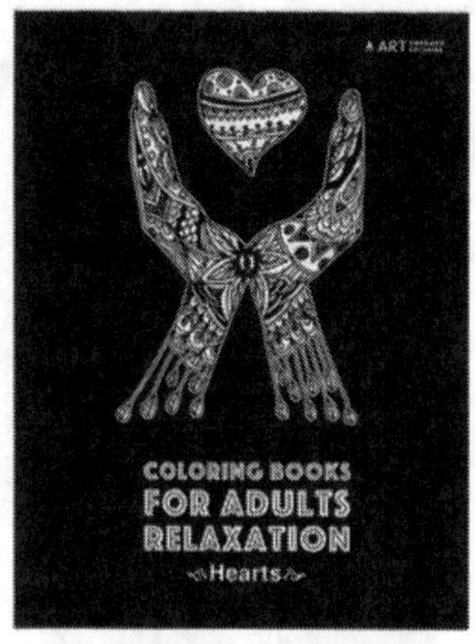

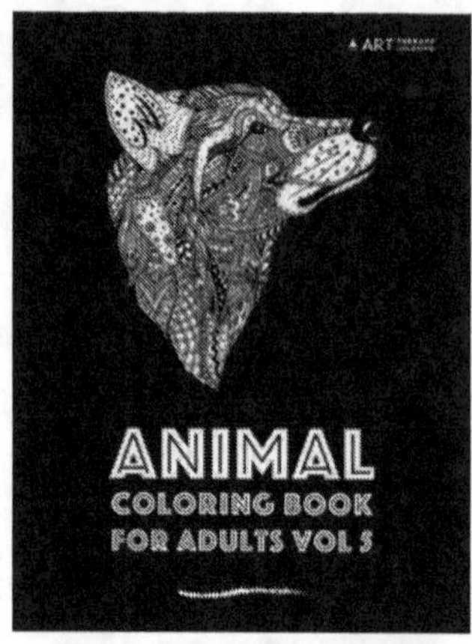

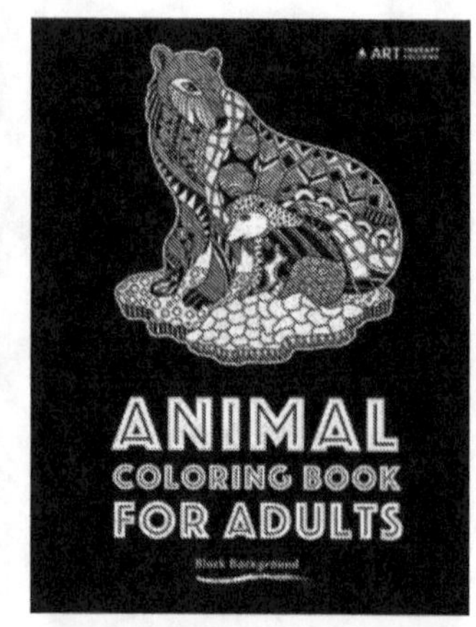

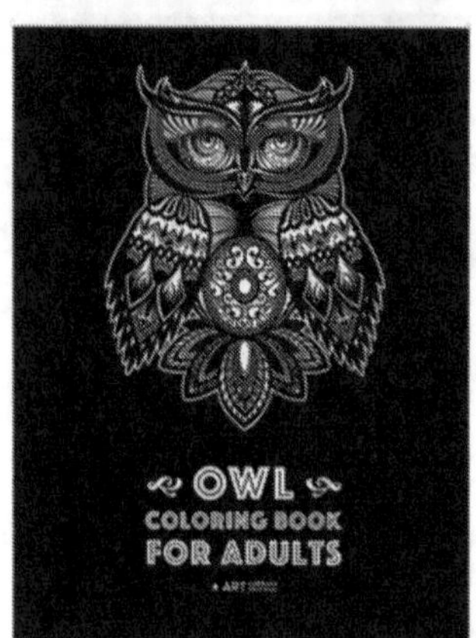

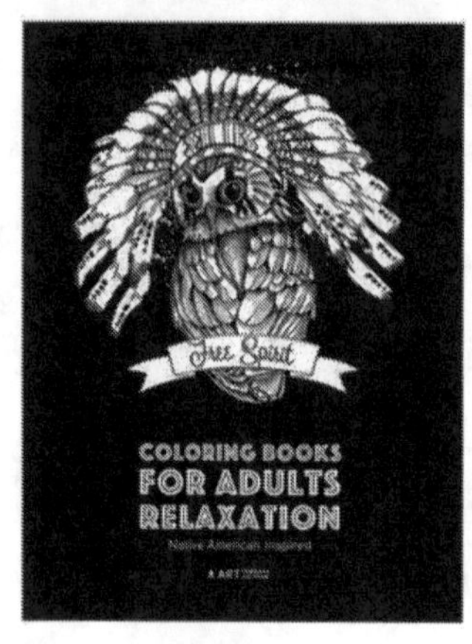

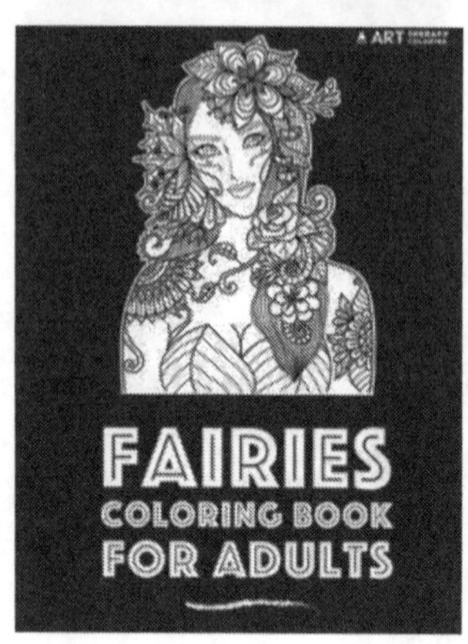

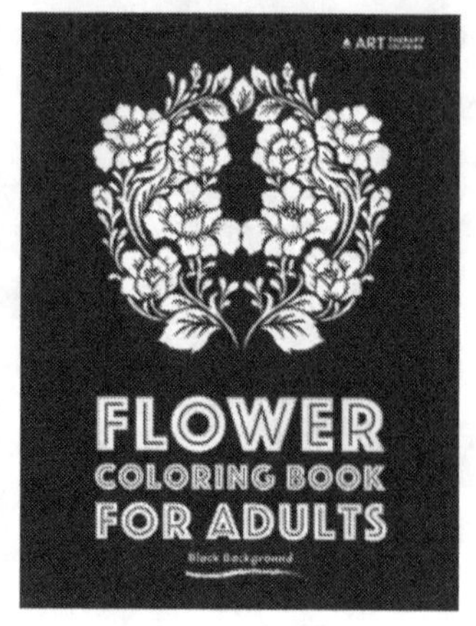

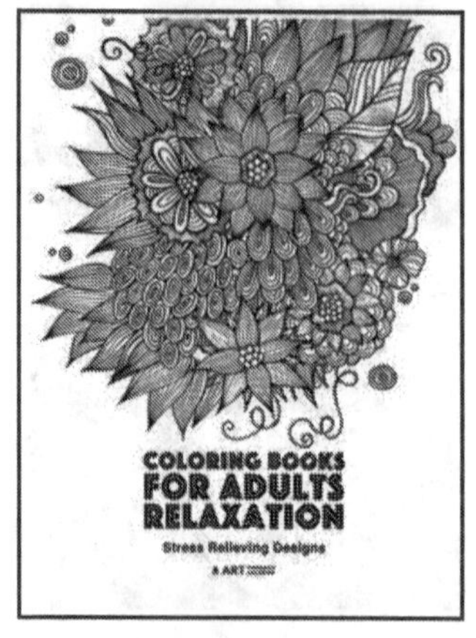

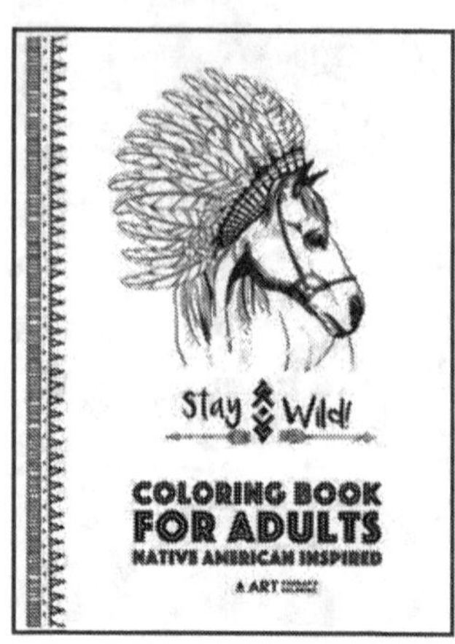

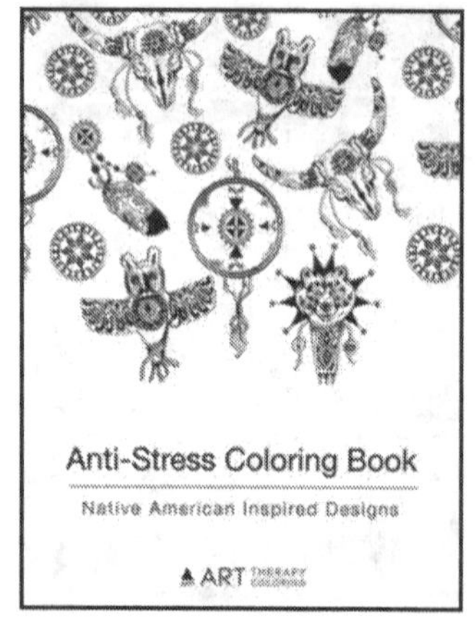

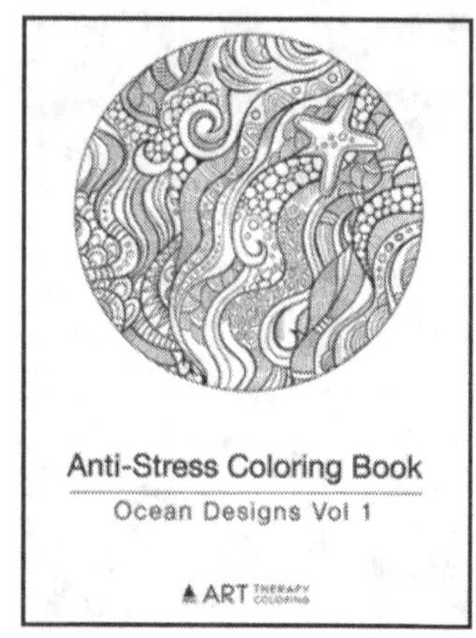

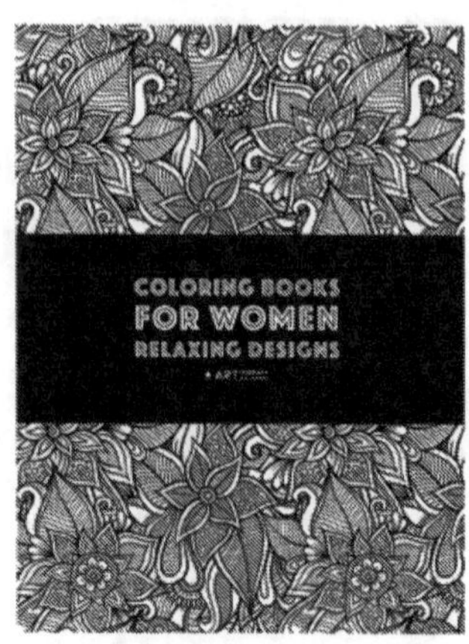

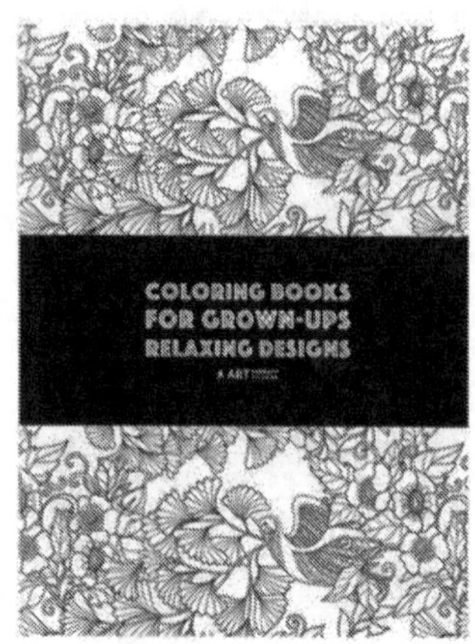

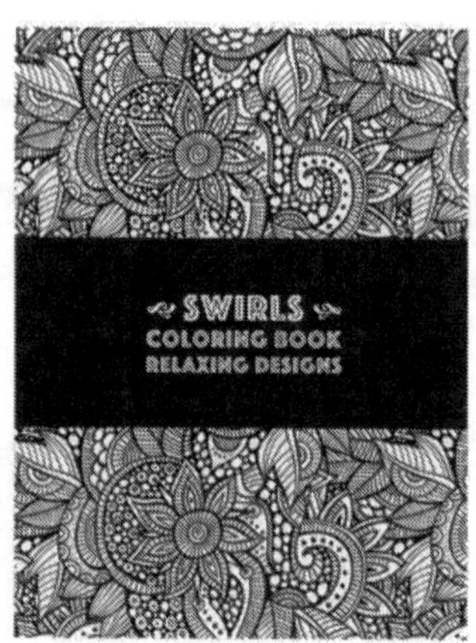

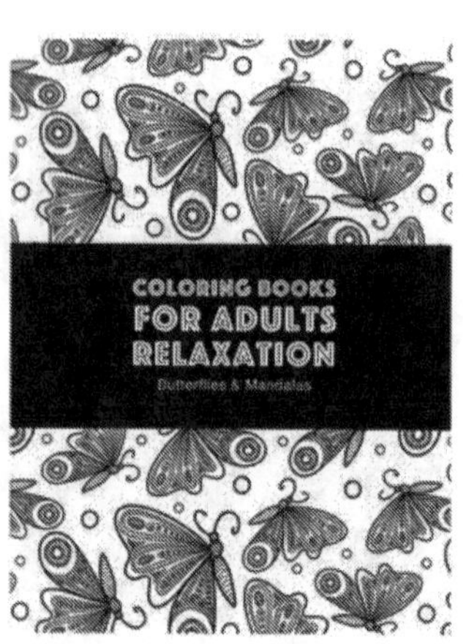

Coloring Books For Men

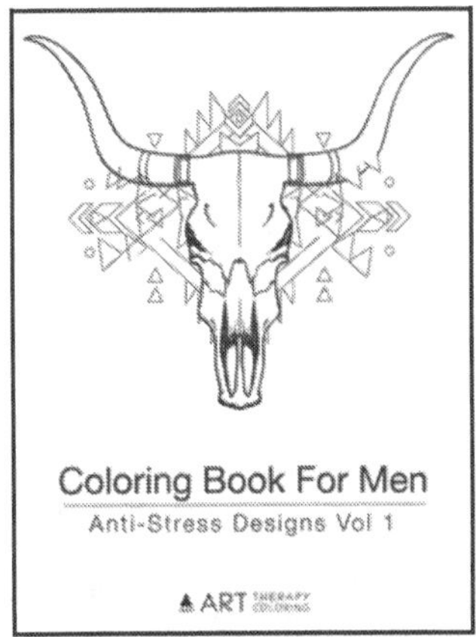
Coloring Book For Men
Anti-Stress Designs Vol 1
ART THERAPY COLORING

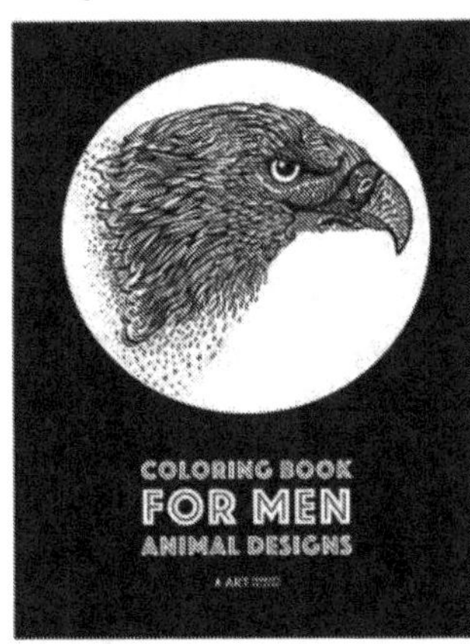
COLORING BOOK
FOR MEN
ANIMAL DESIGNS

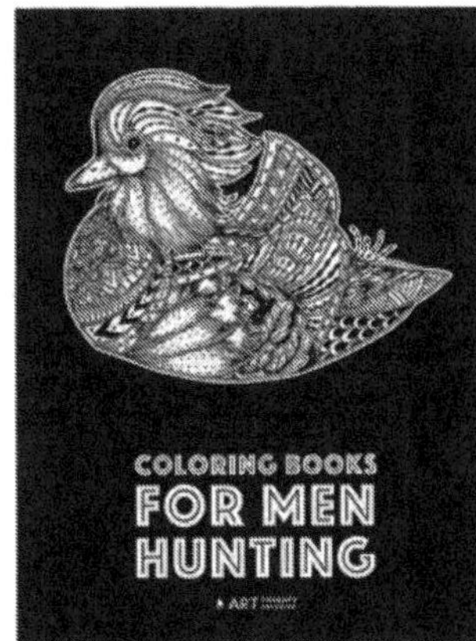
COLORING BOOKS
FOR MEN
HUNTING

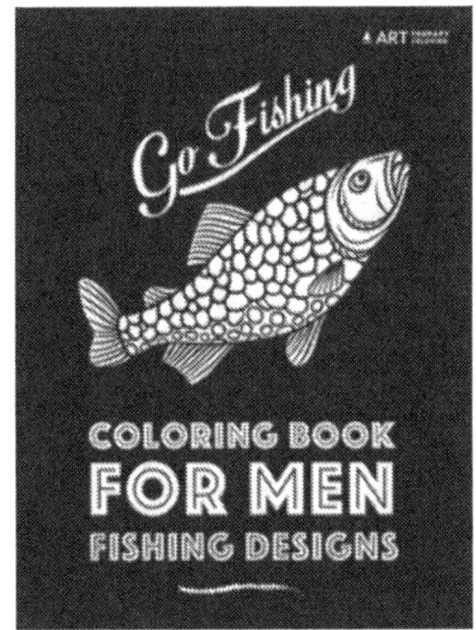
Go Fishing
COLORING BOOK
FOR MEN
FISHING DESIGNS

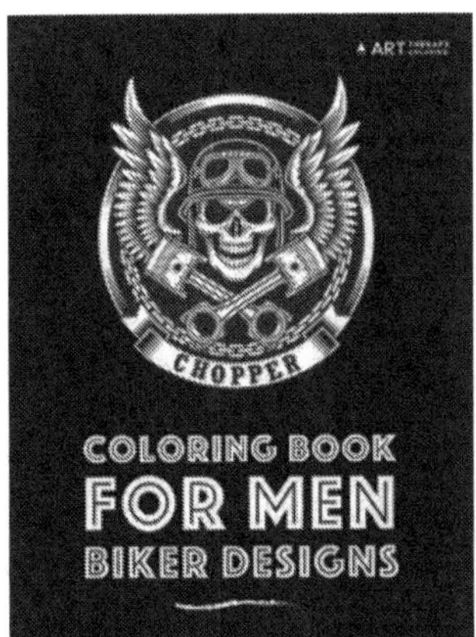
CHOPPER
COLORING BOOK
FOR MEN
BIKER DESIGNS

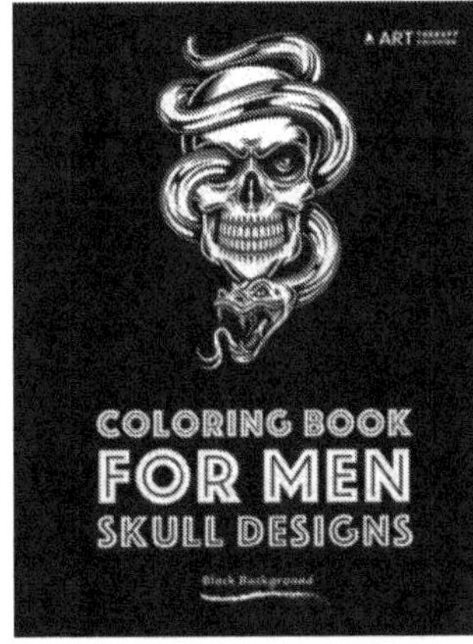
COLORING BOOK
FOR MEN
SKULL DESIGNS
Black Background

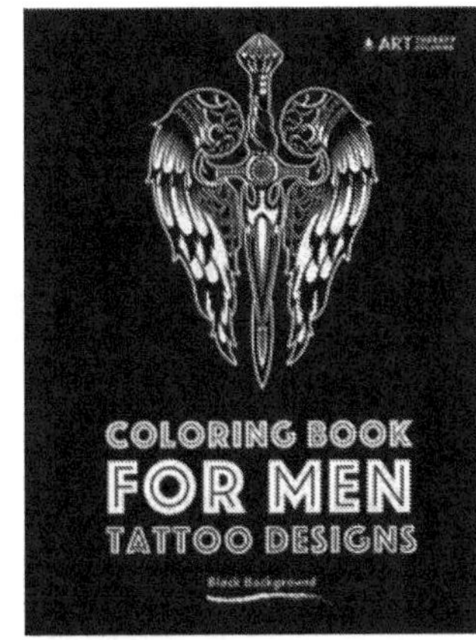
COLORING BOOK
FOR MEN
TATTOO DESIGNS
Black Background

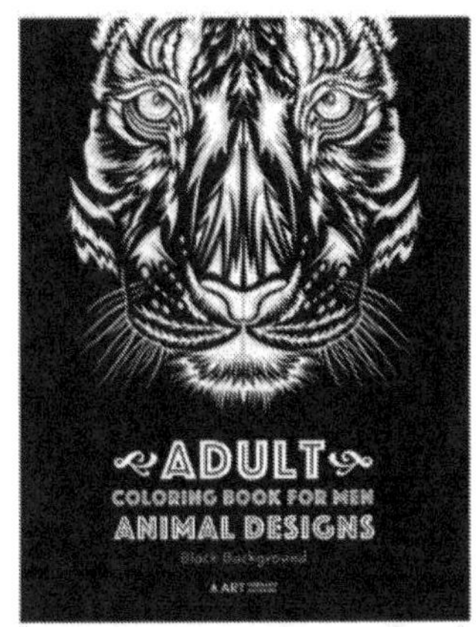
ADULT
COLORING BOOK FOR MEN
ANIMAL DESIGNS

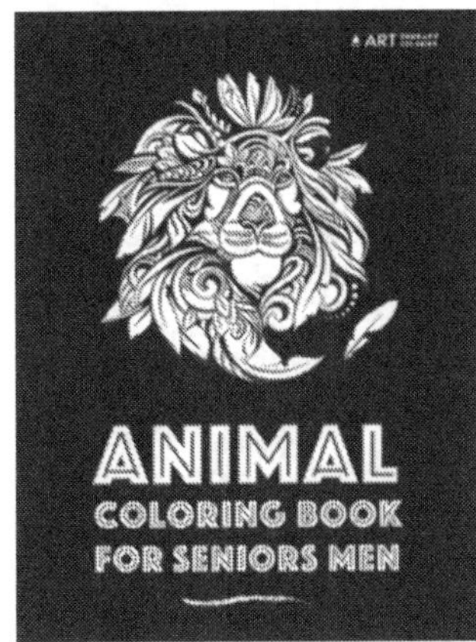
ANIMAL
COLORING BOOK
FOR SENIORS MEN

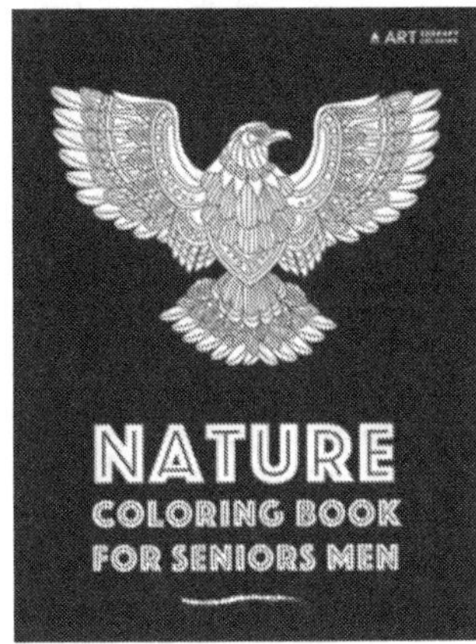
NATURE
COLORING BOOK
FOR SENIORS MEN

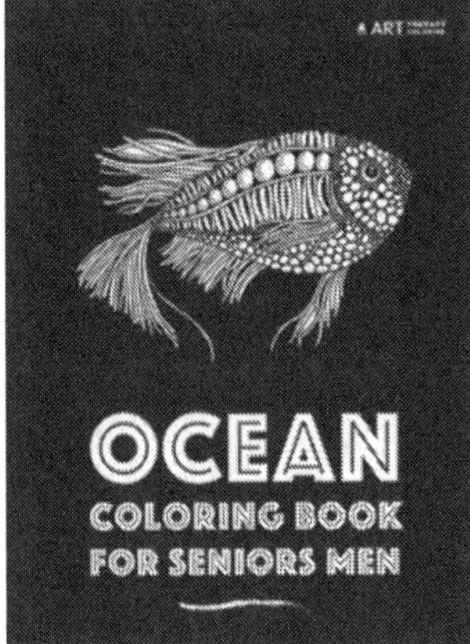
OCEAN
COLORING BOOK
FOR SENIORS MEN

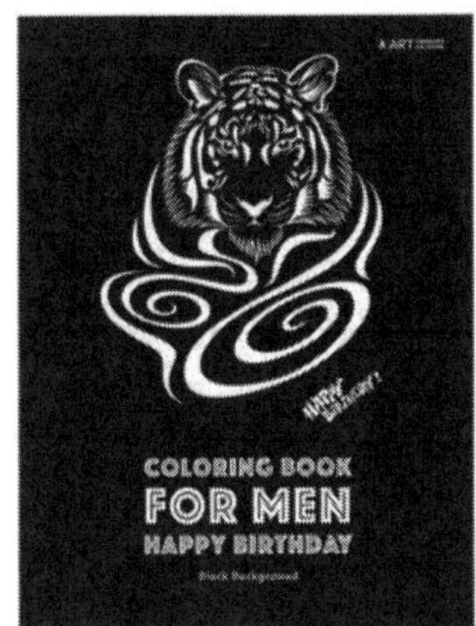
COLORING BOOK
FOR MEN
HAPPY BIRTHDAY
Black Background

Coloring Books For Teens

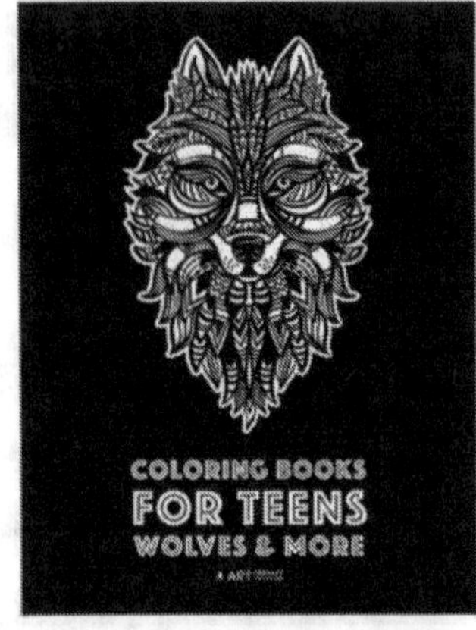

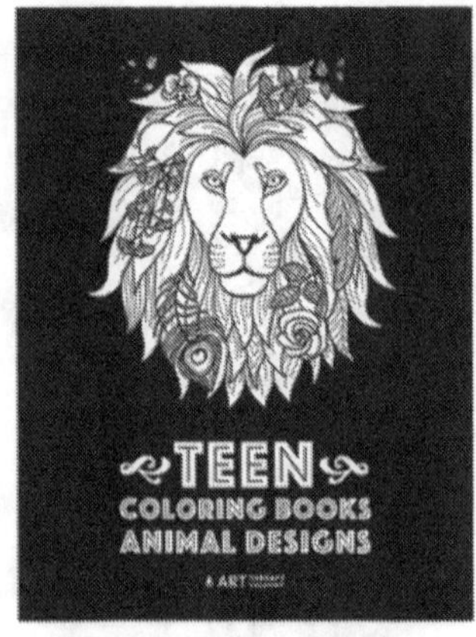

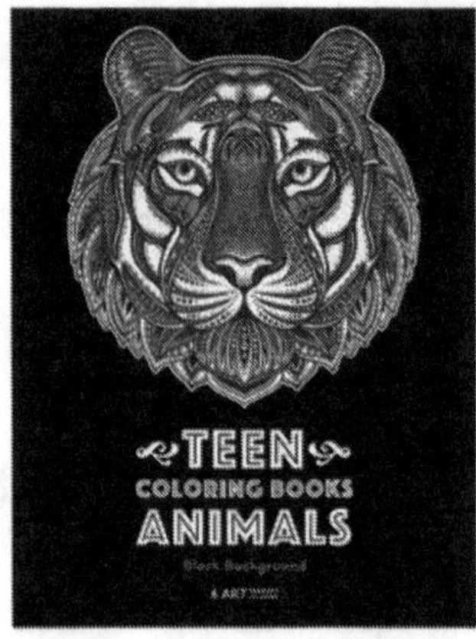

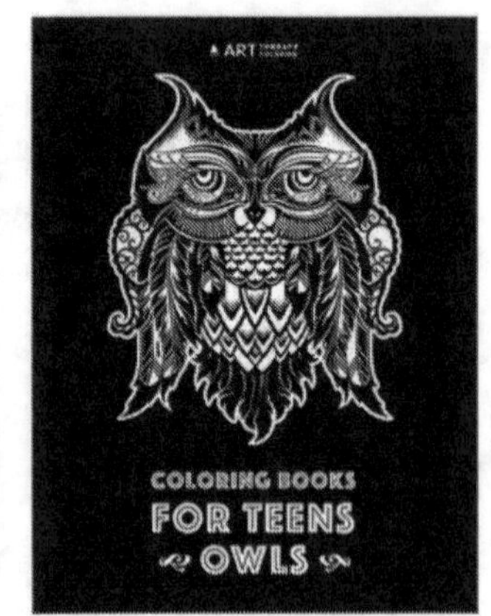

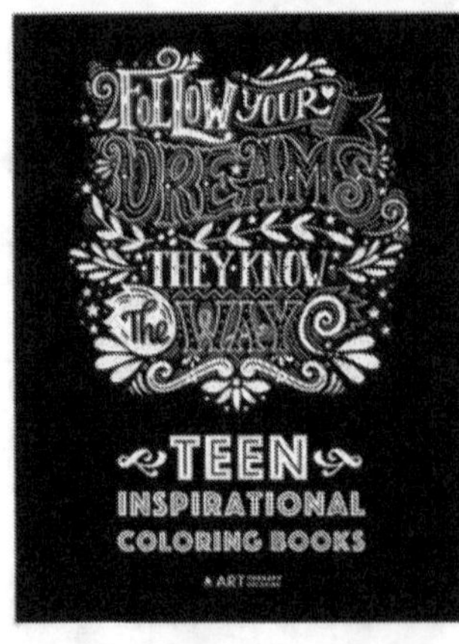

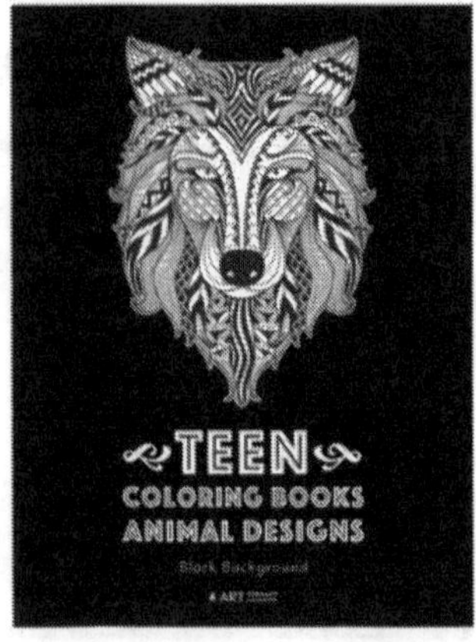

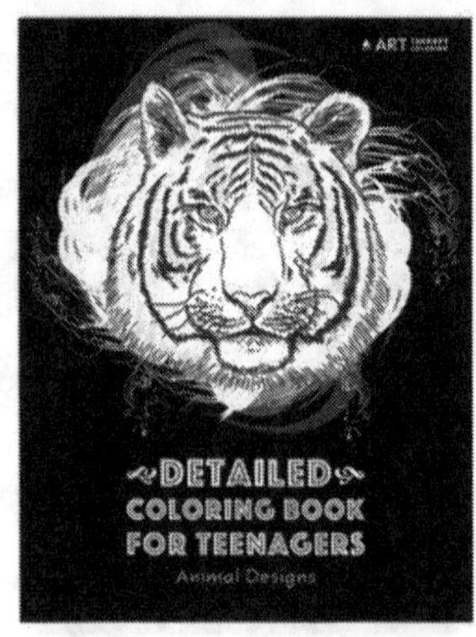

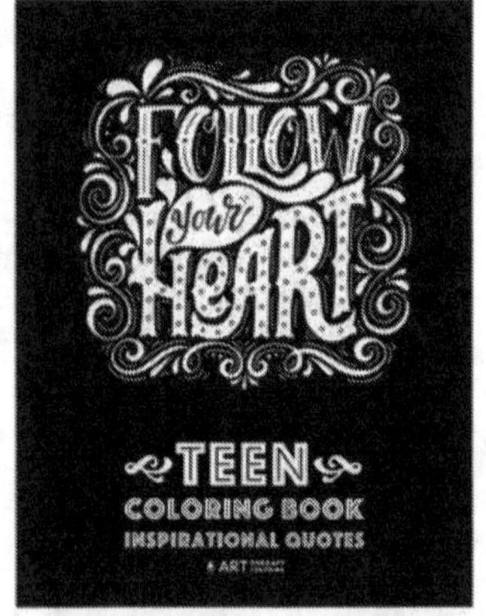

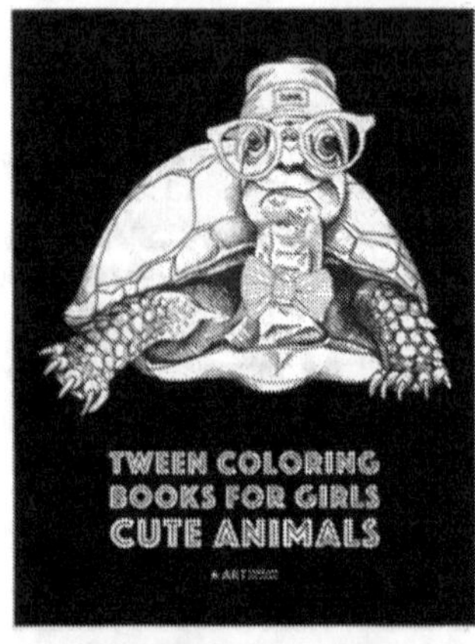

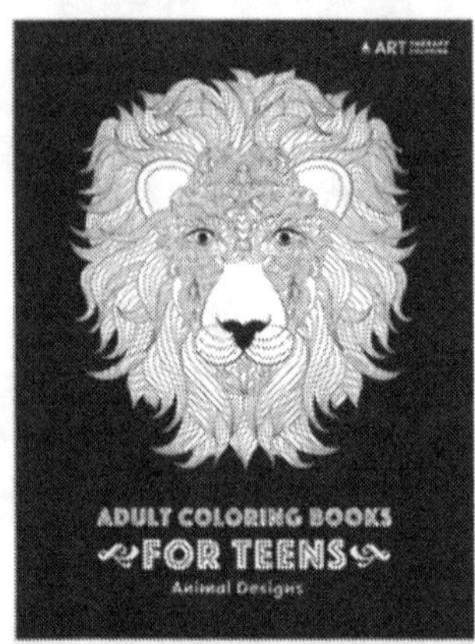

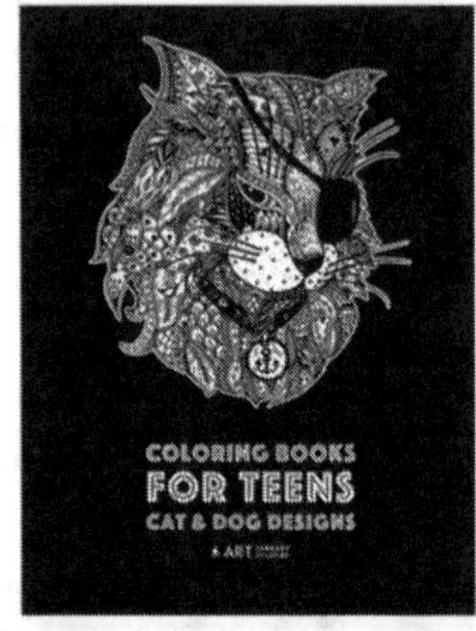

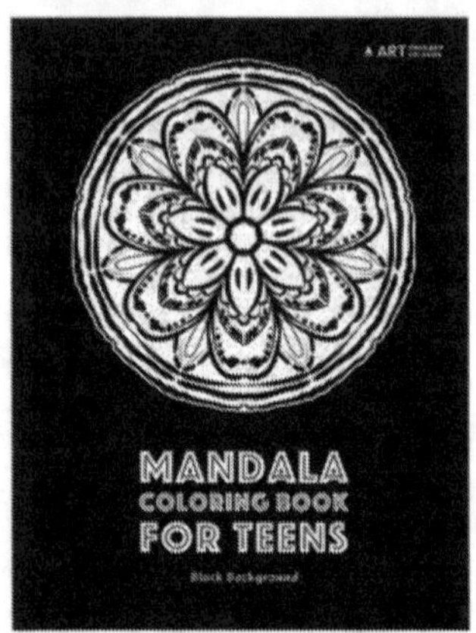

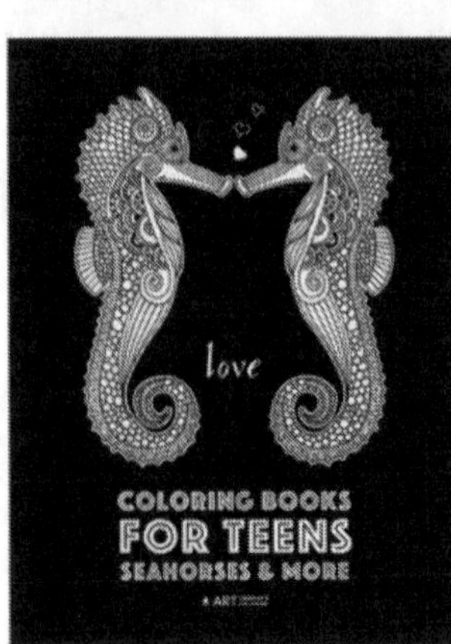

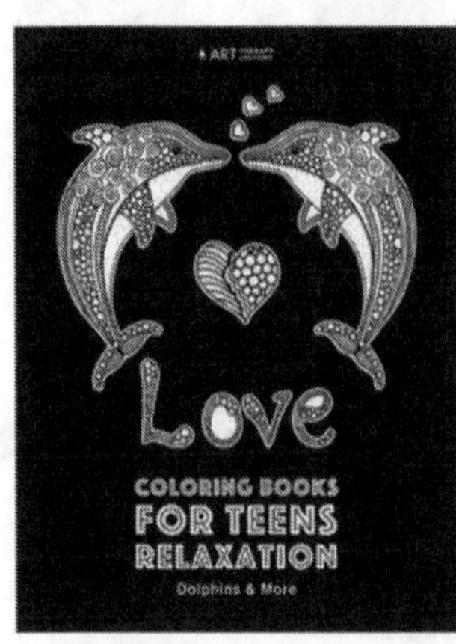

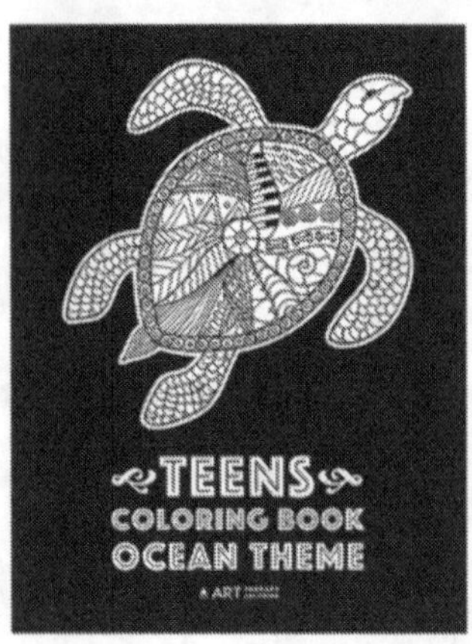

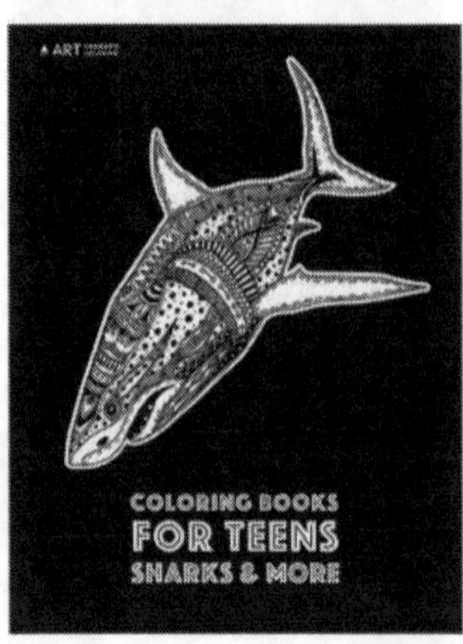

Coloring Books For Teens

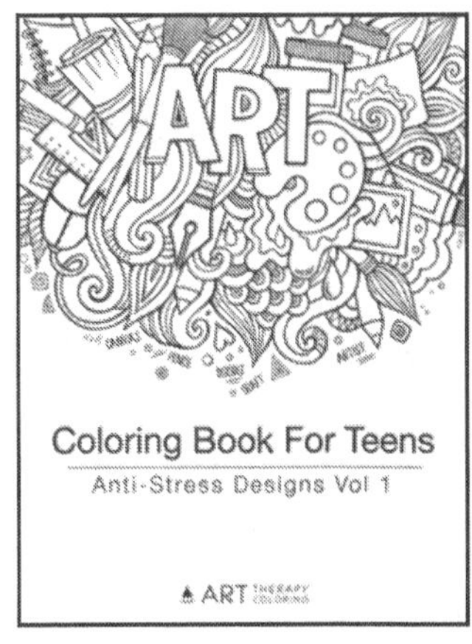

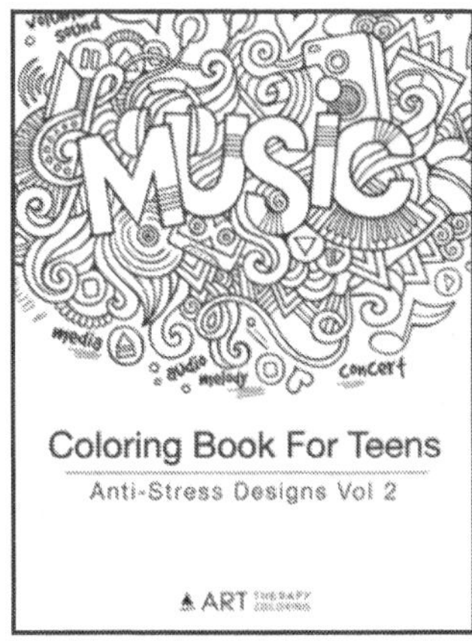

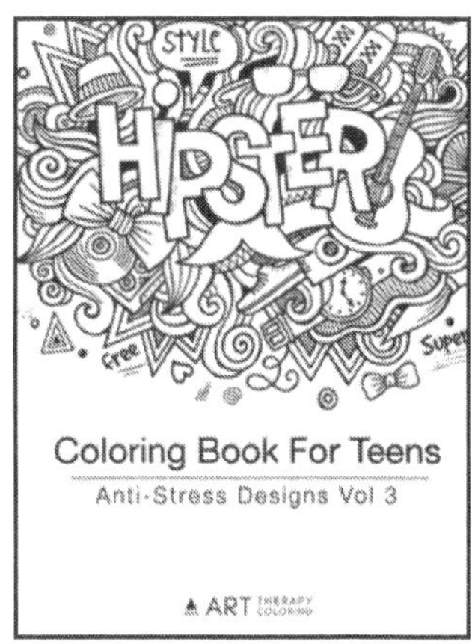

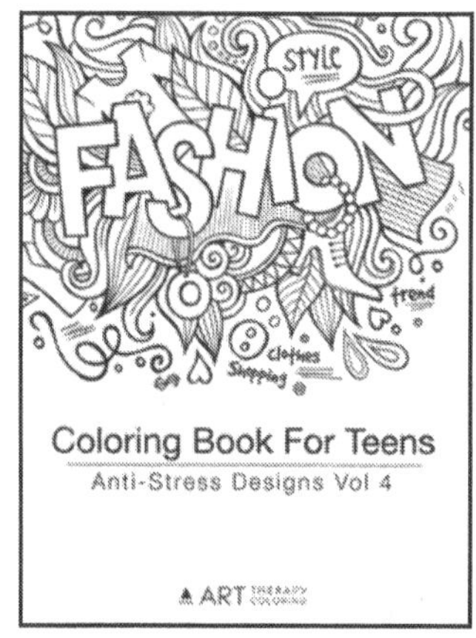

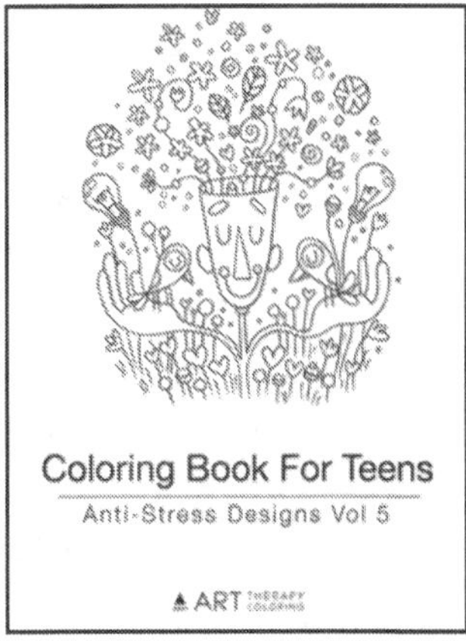

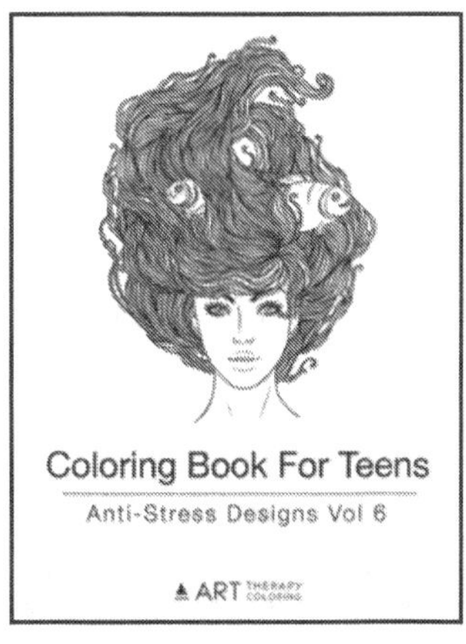

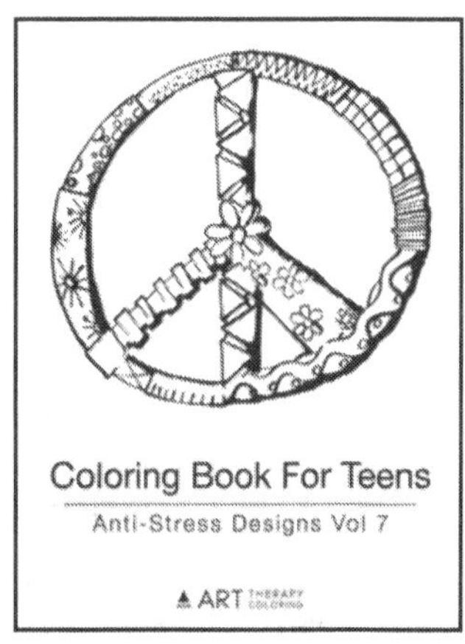

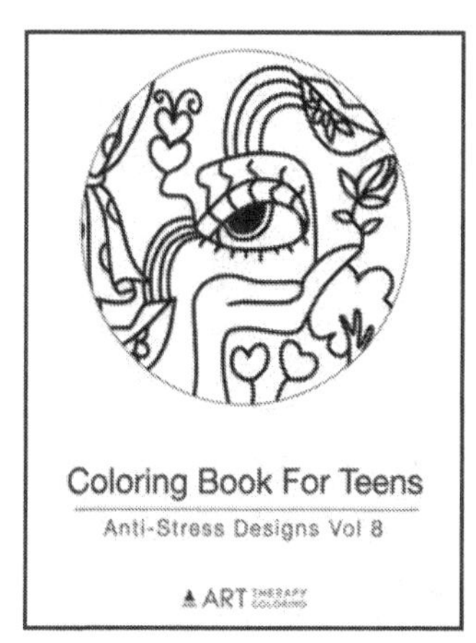

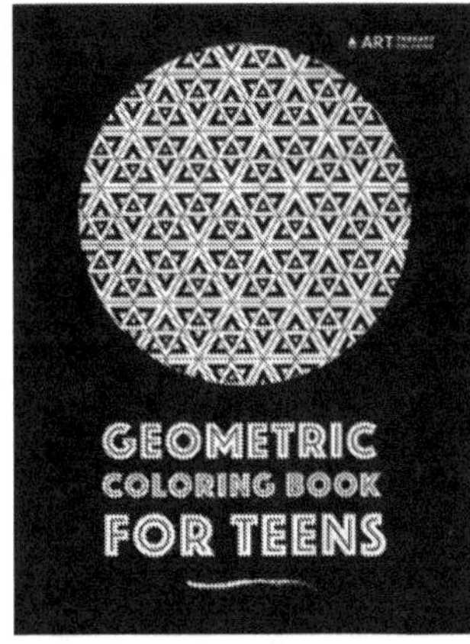

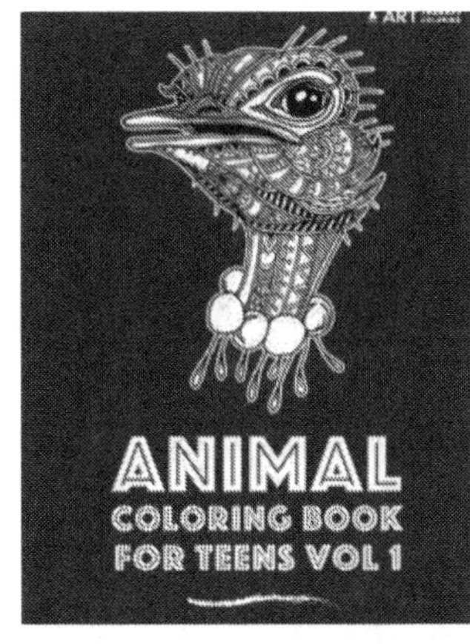

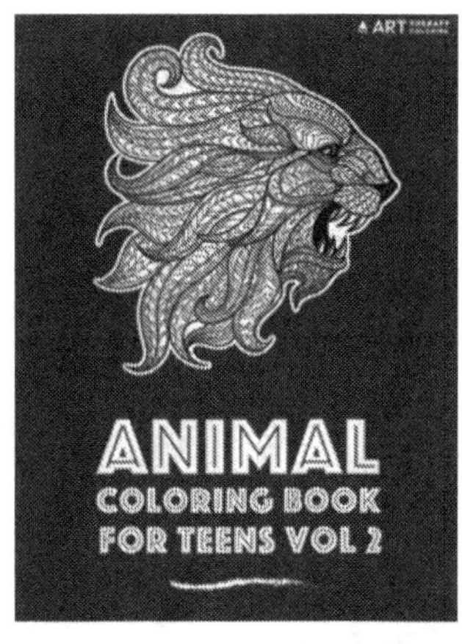

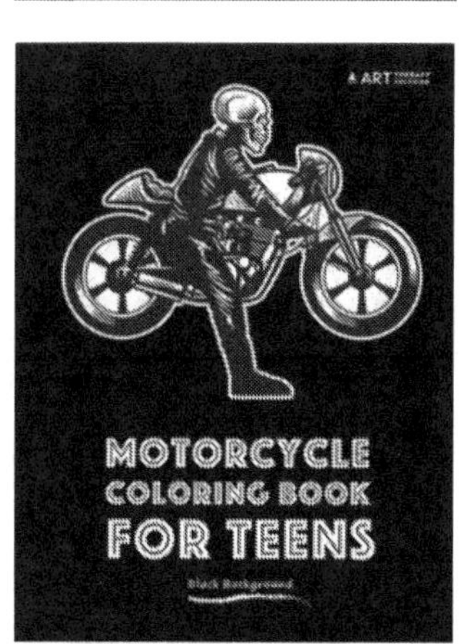

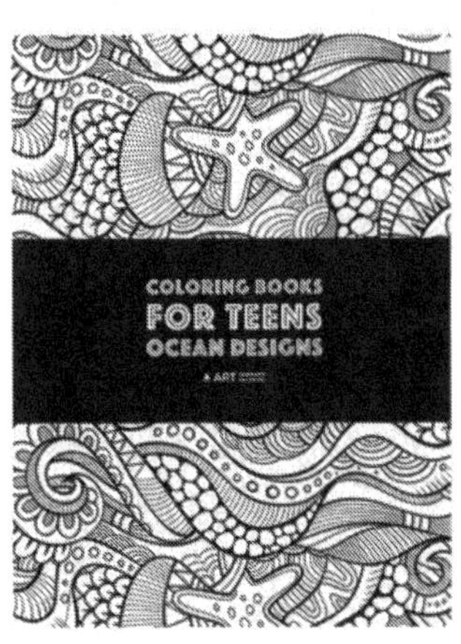

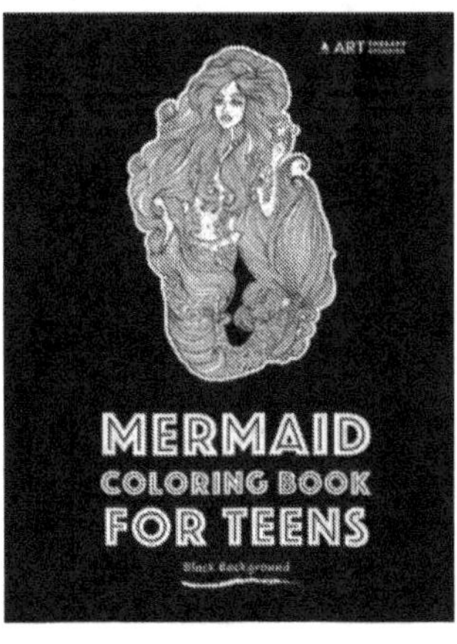

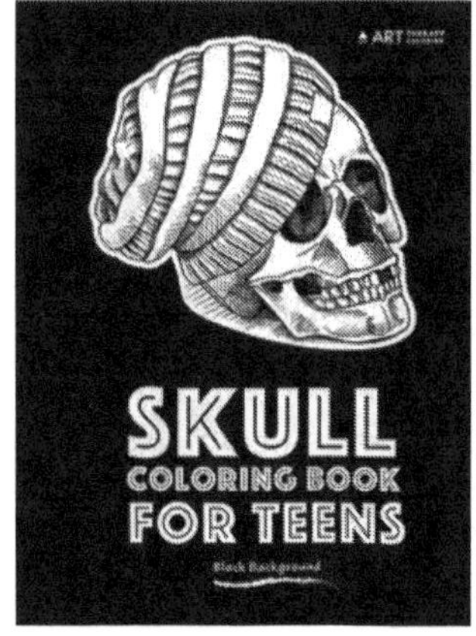

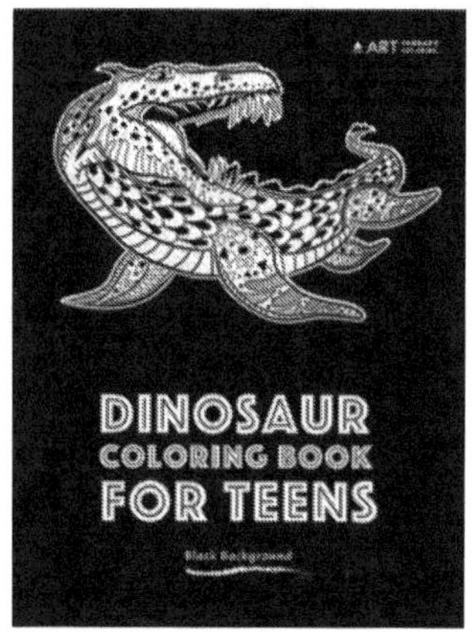

Coloring Books For Girls

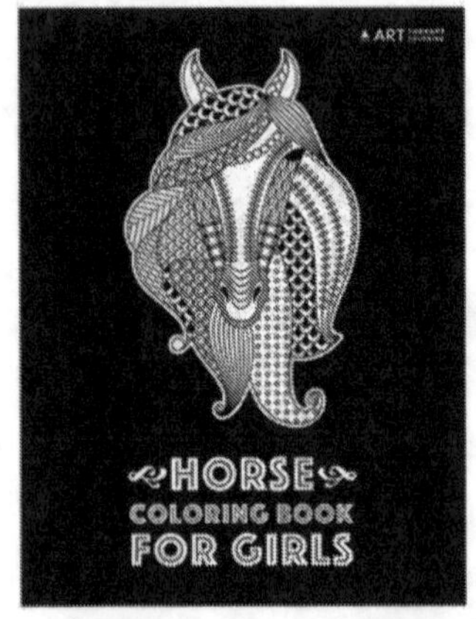

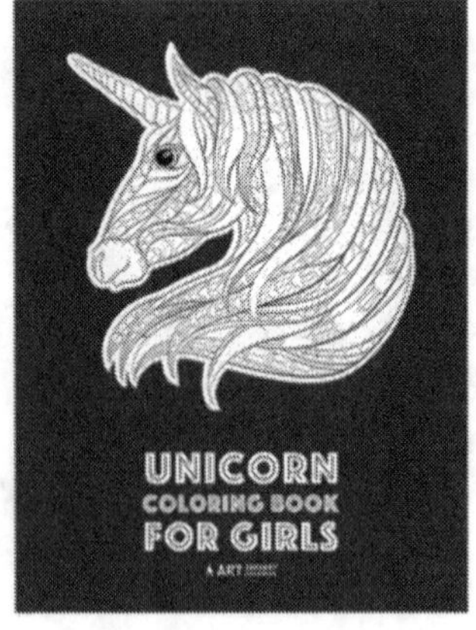

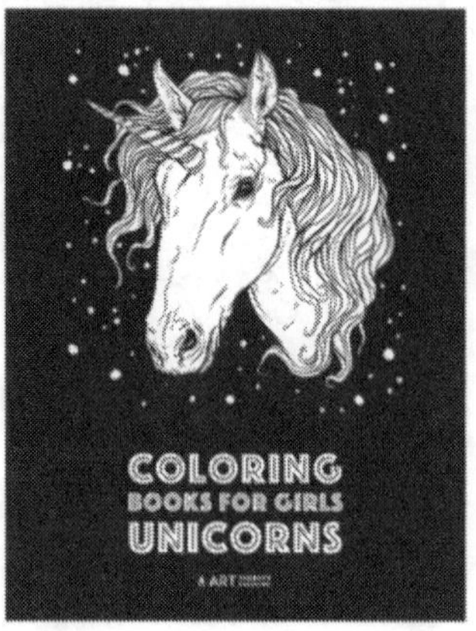

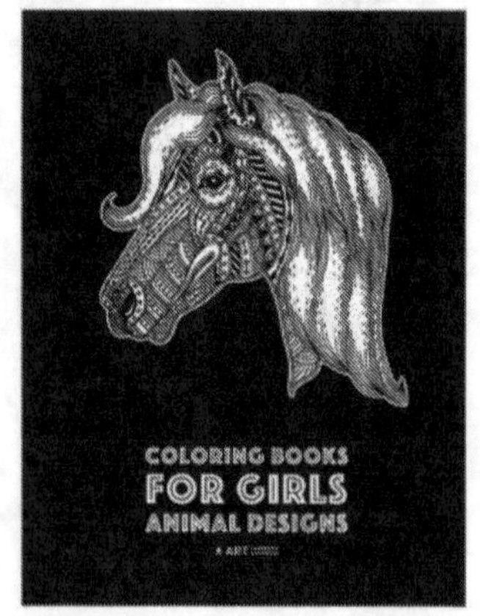

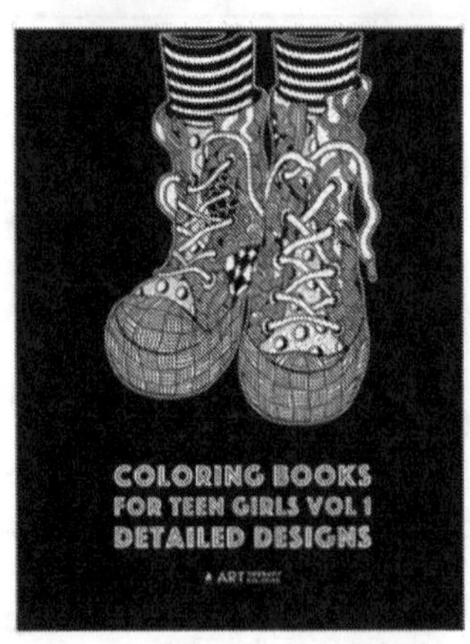

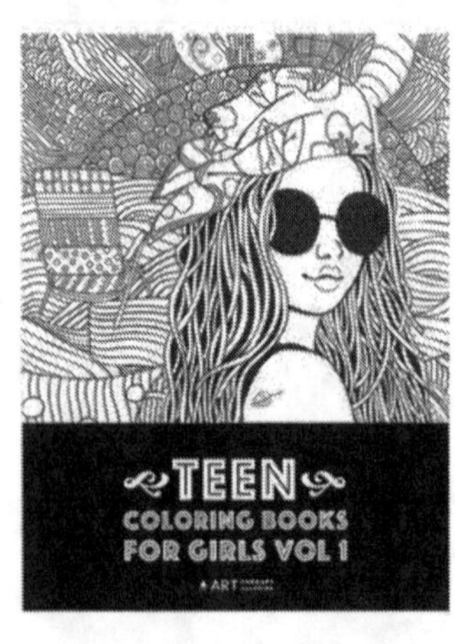

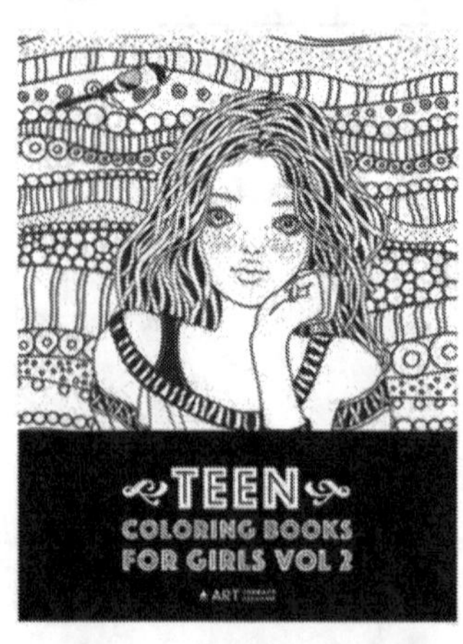

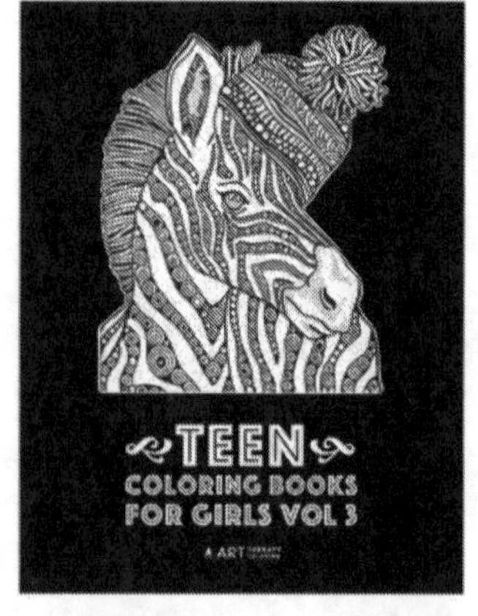

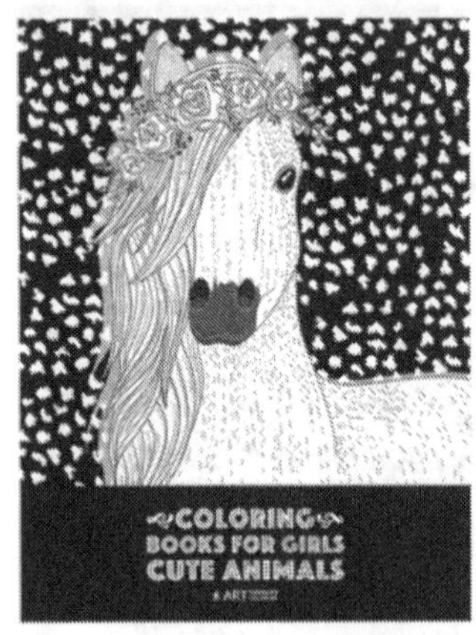

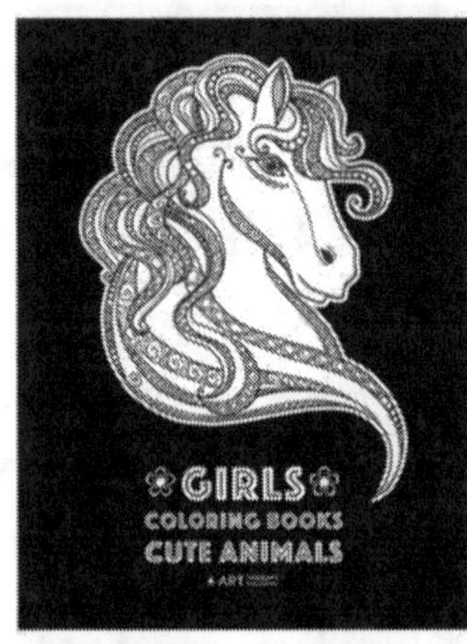

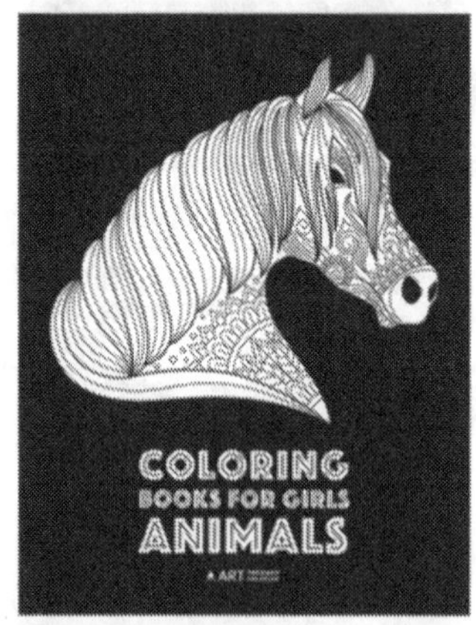

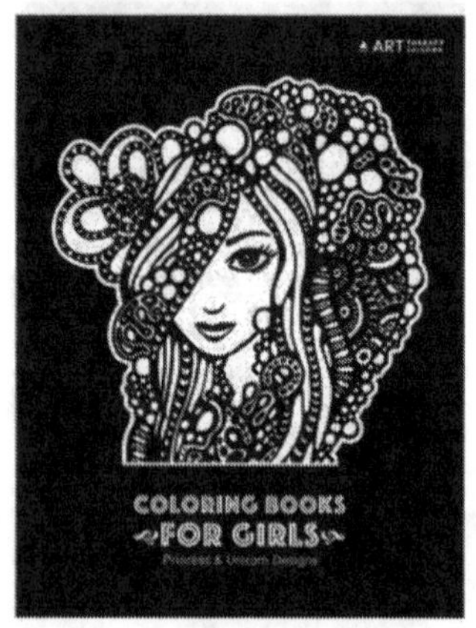

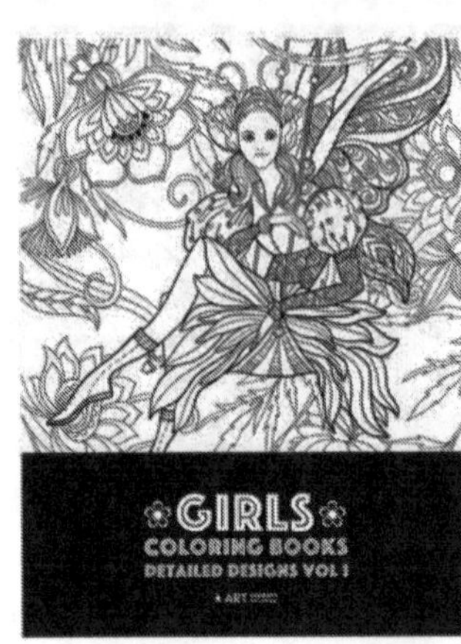

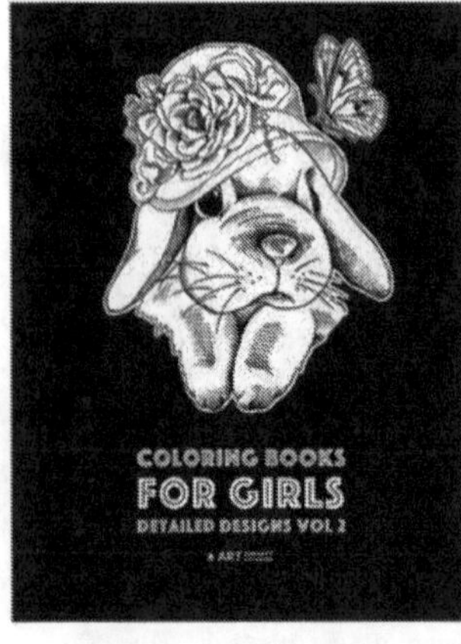

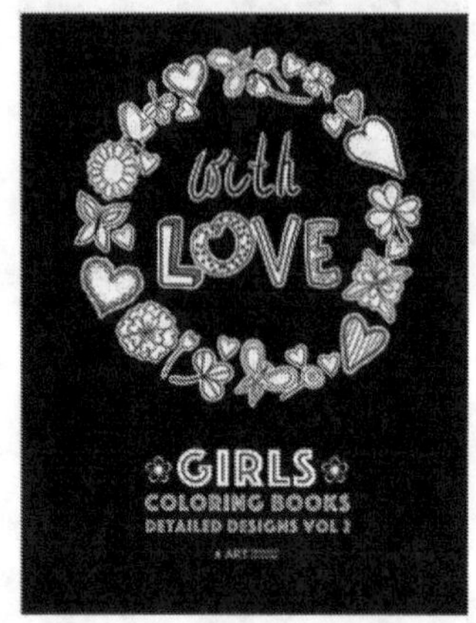

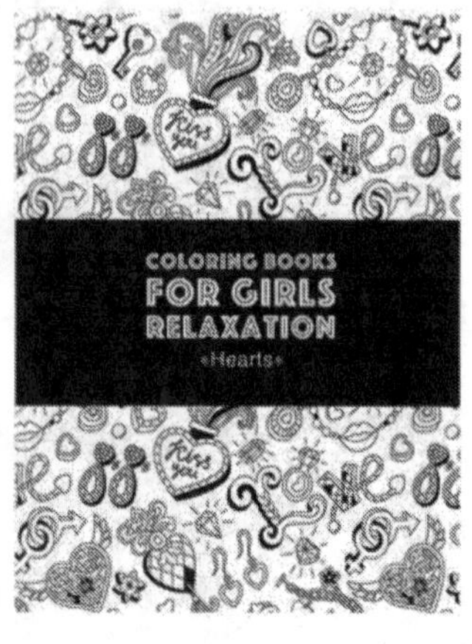

Art Therapy Coloring Books

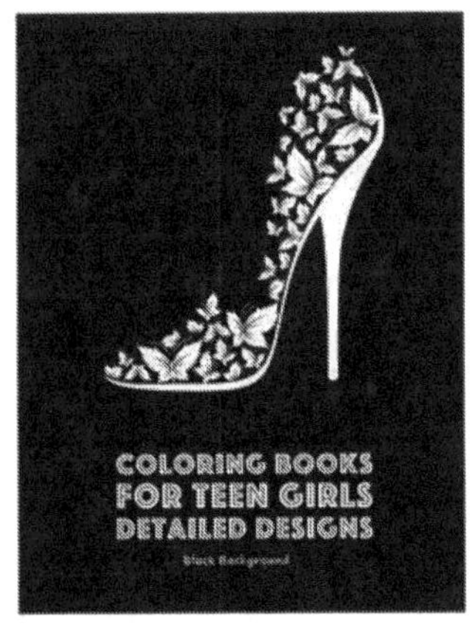

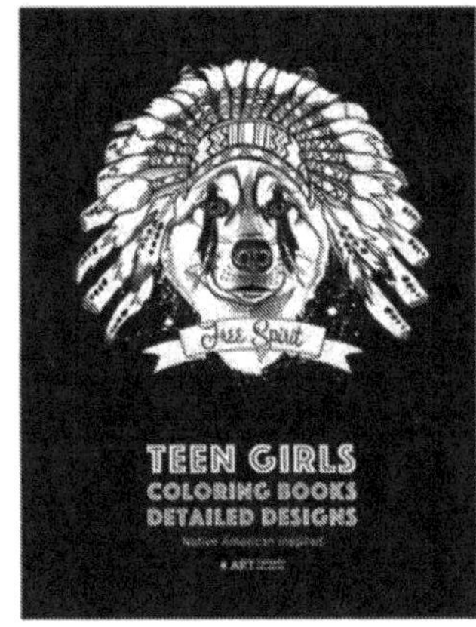

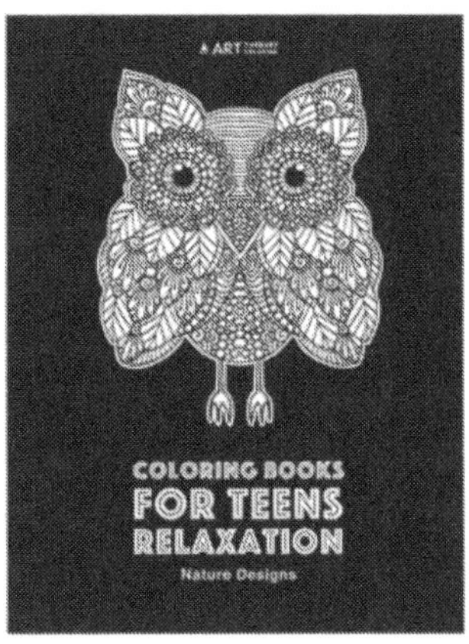

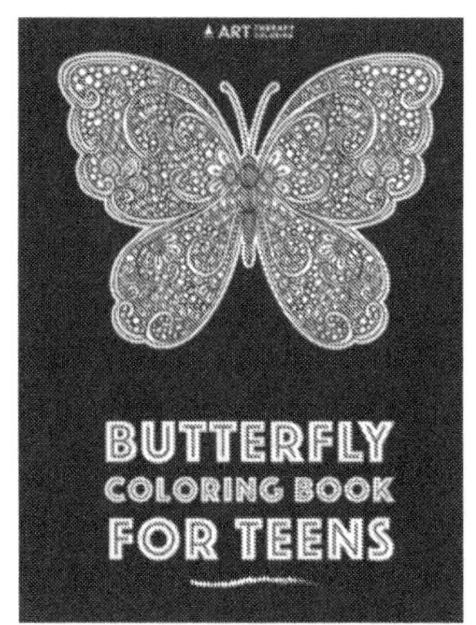

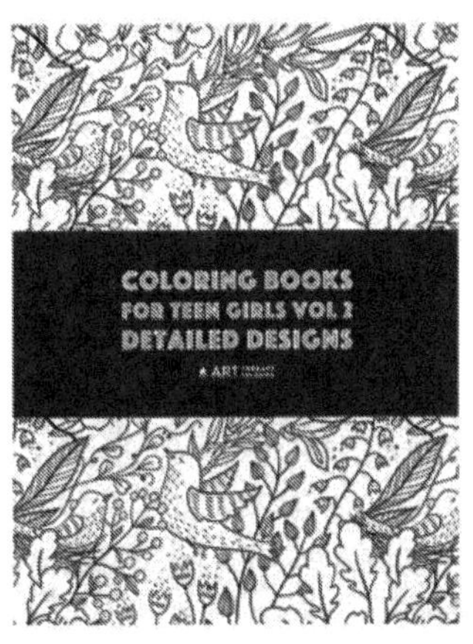

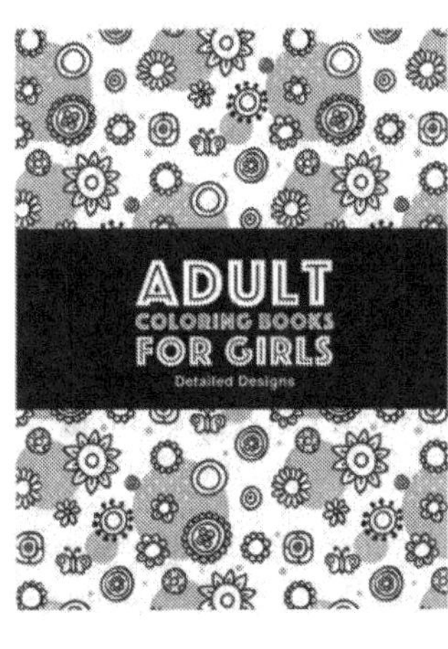

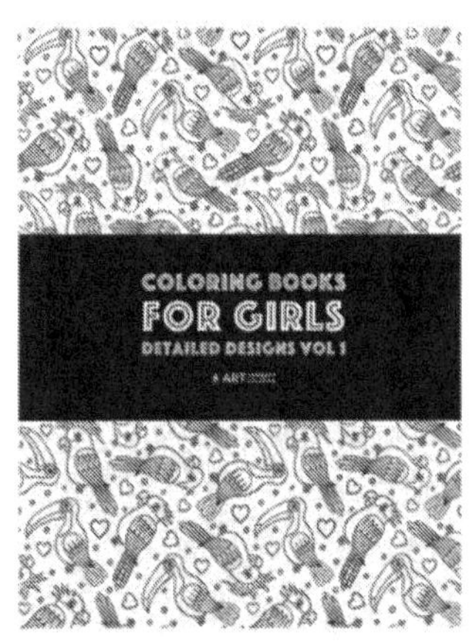

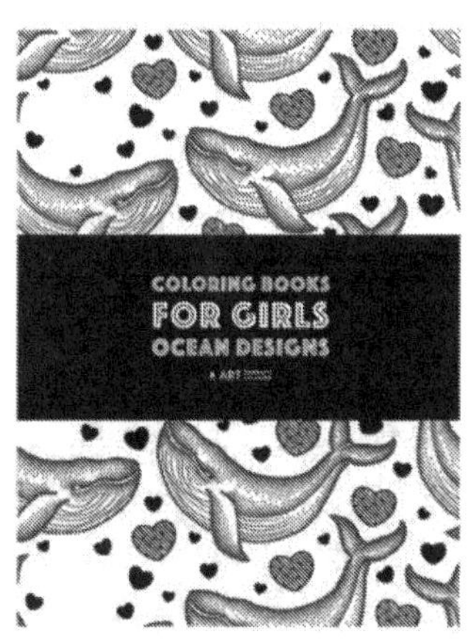

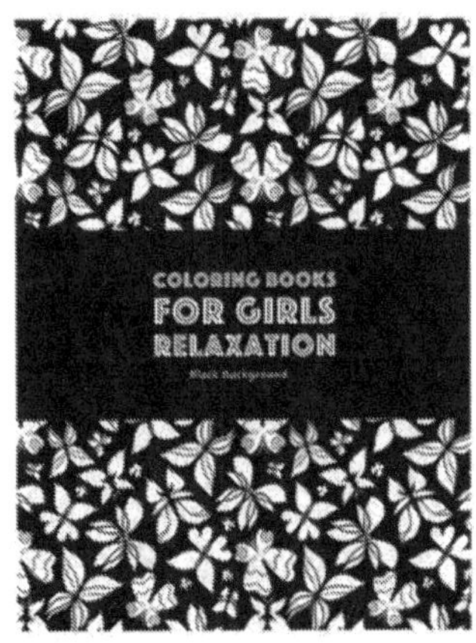

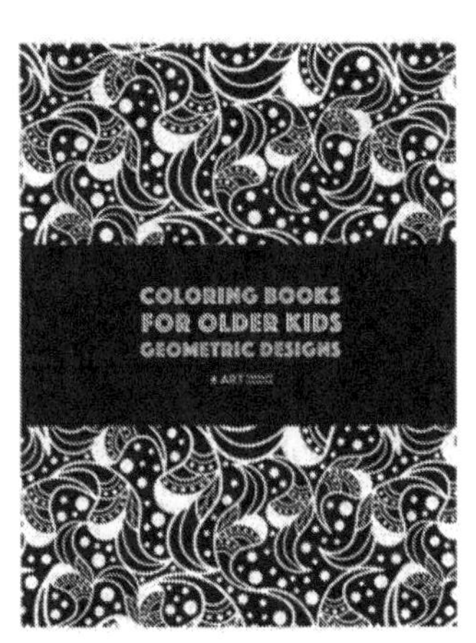

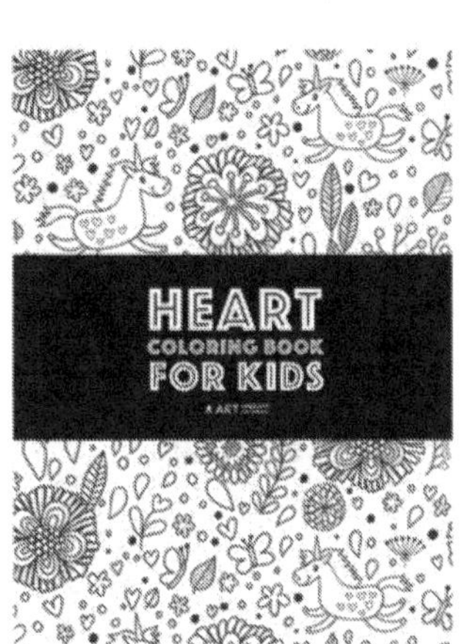

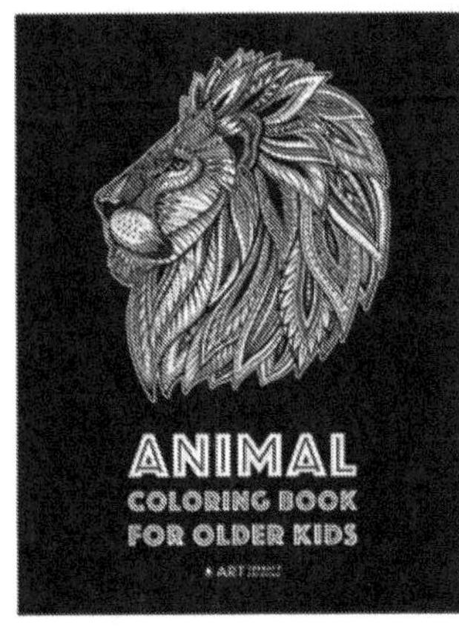

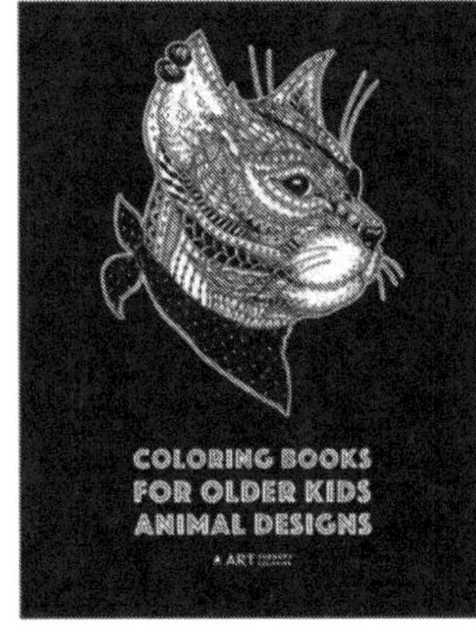

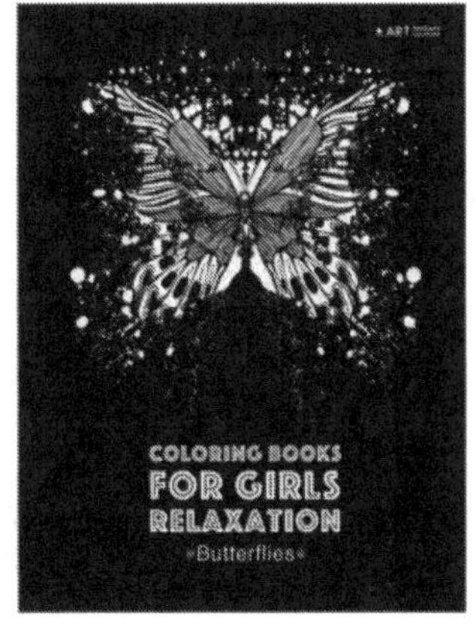

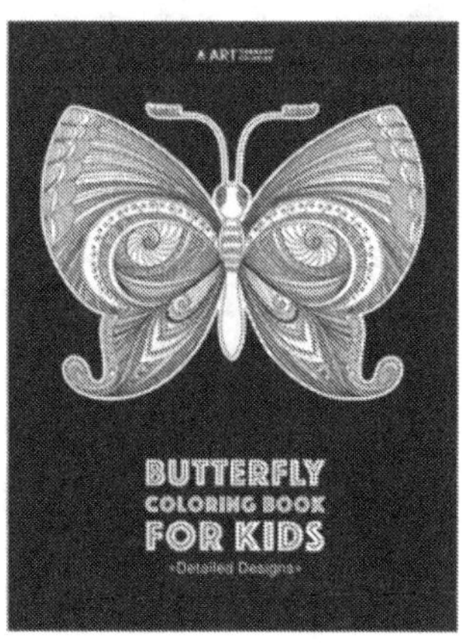

Coloring Books For Boys

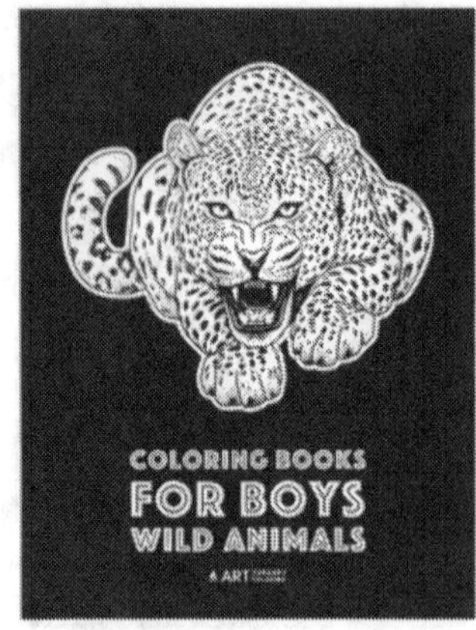
COLORING BOOKS
FOR BOYS
WILD ANIMALS

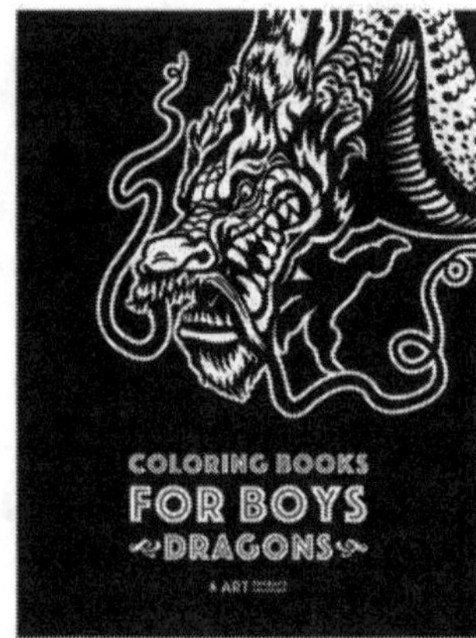
COLORING BOOKS
FOR BOYS
DRAGONS

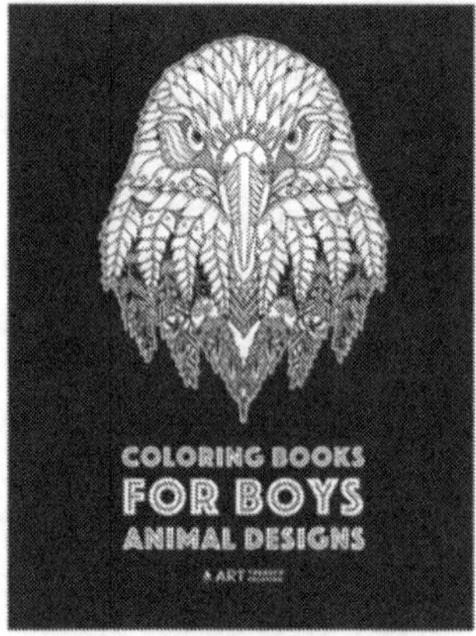
COLORING BOOKS
FOR BOYS
ANIMAL DESIGNS

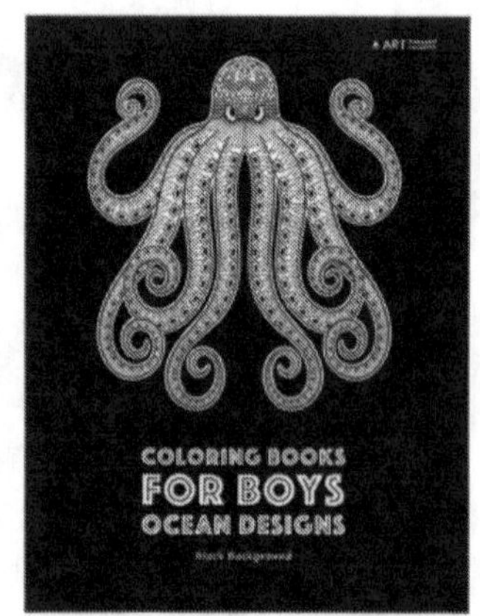
COLORING BOOKS
FOR BOYS
OCEAN DESIGNS
Black Background

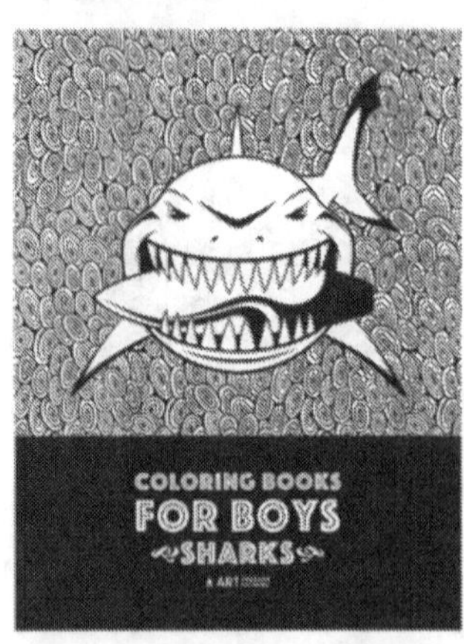
COLORING BOOKS
FOR BOYS
SHARKS

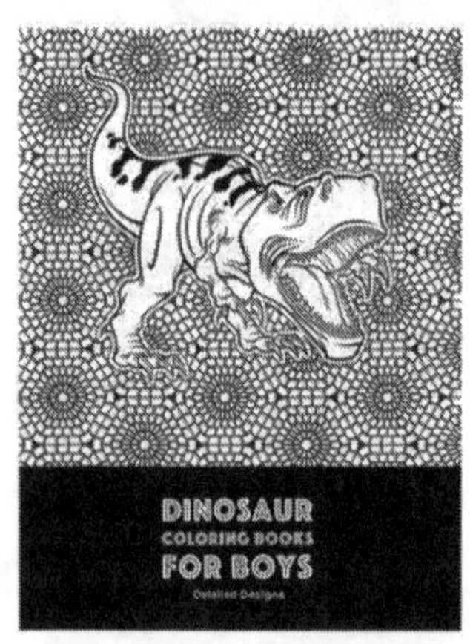
DINOSAUR
COLORING BOOKS
FOR BOYS
Detailed Designs

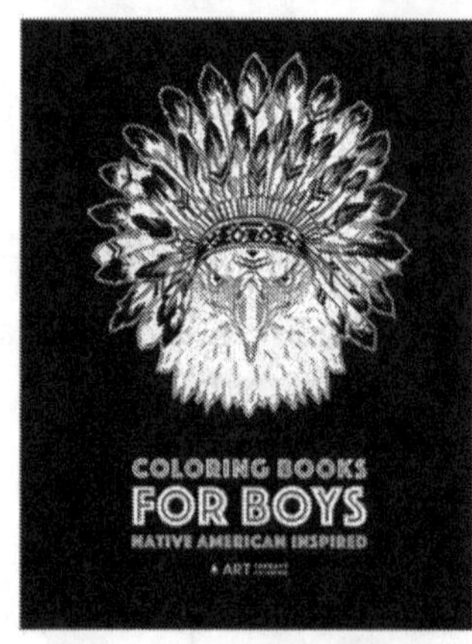
COLORING BOOKS
FOR BOYS
NATIVE AMERICAN INSPIRED

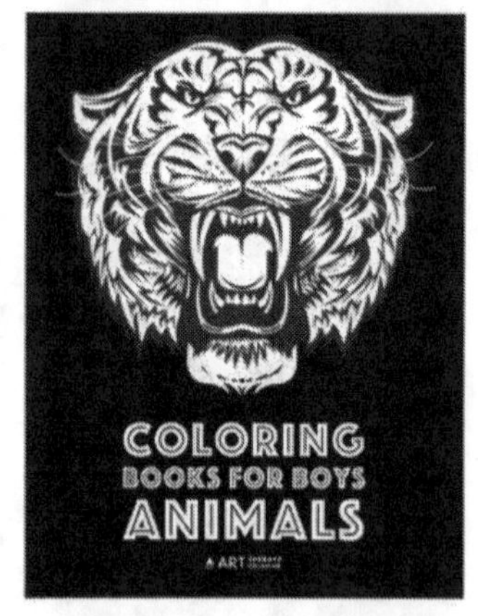
COLORING
BOOKS FOR BOYS
ANIMALS

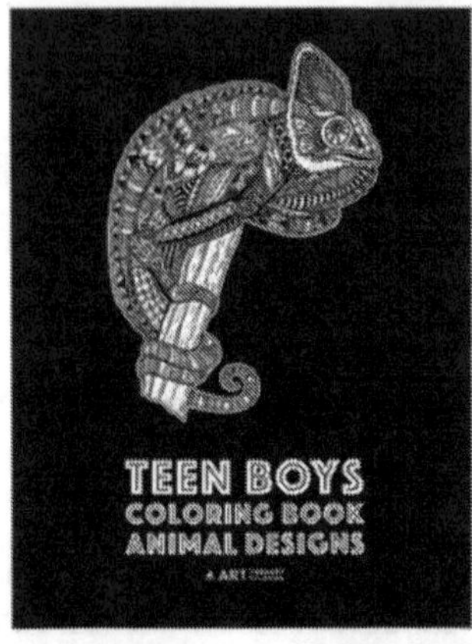
TEEN BOYS
COLORING BOOK
ANIMAL DESIGNS

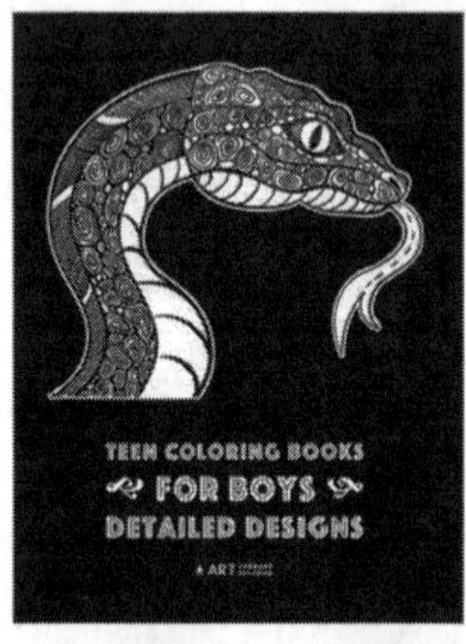
TEEN COLORING BOOKS
FOR BOYS
DETAILED DESIGNS

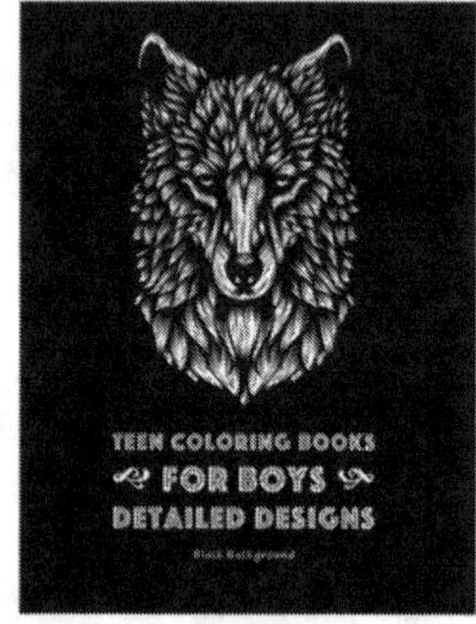
TEEN COLORING BOOKS
FOR BOYS
DETAILED DESIGNS
Black Background

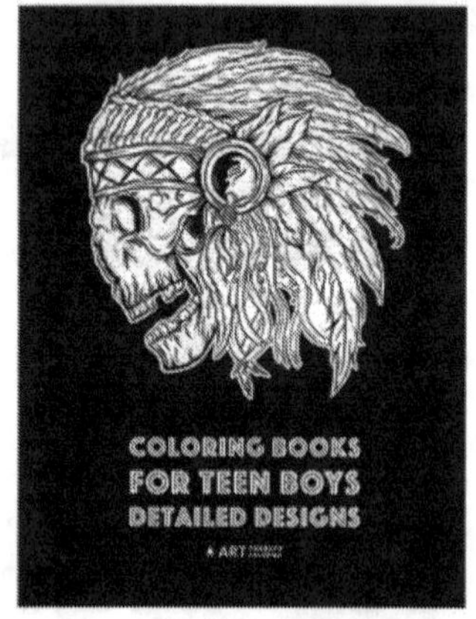
COLORING BOOKS
FOR TEEN BOYS
DETAILED DESIGNS

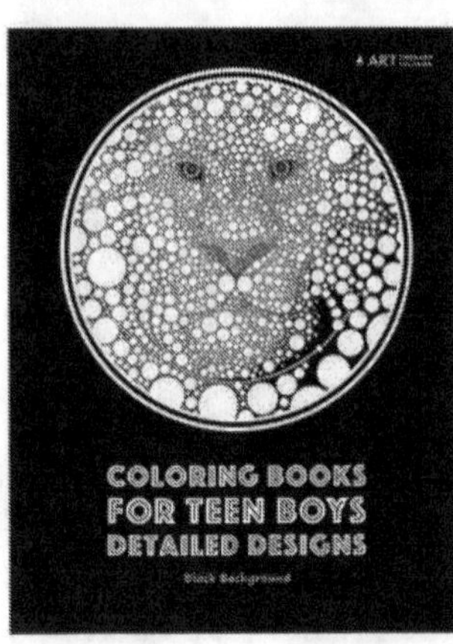
COLORING BOOKS
FOR TEEN BOYS
DETAILED DESIGNS
Black Background

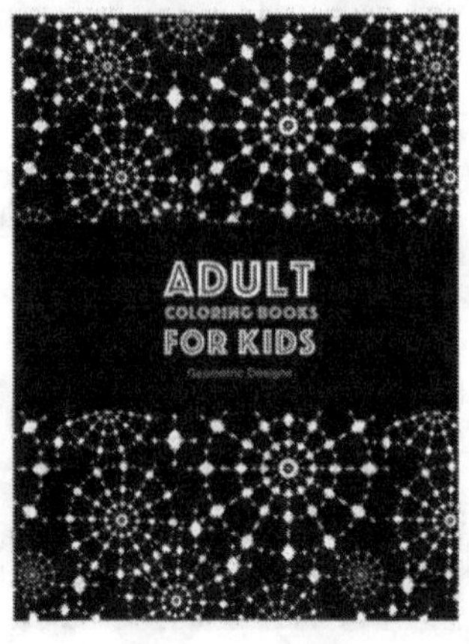
ADULT
COLORING BOOKS
FOR KIDS
Geometric Designs

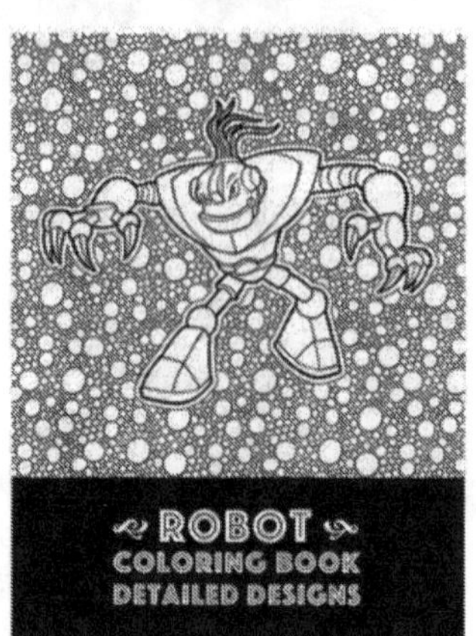
ROBOT
COLORING BOOK
DETAILED DESIGNS

DETAILED
COLORING BOOKS
FOR KIDS
Geometric Designs

Coloring Books For Kids

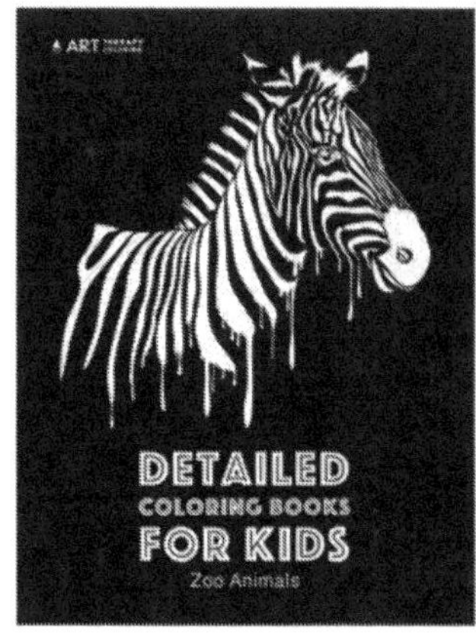
DETAILED
COLORING BOOKS
FOR KIDS
Zoo Animals

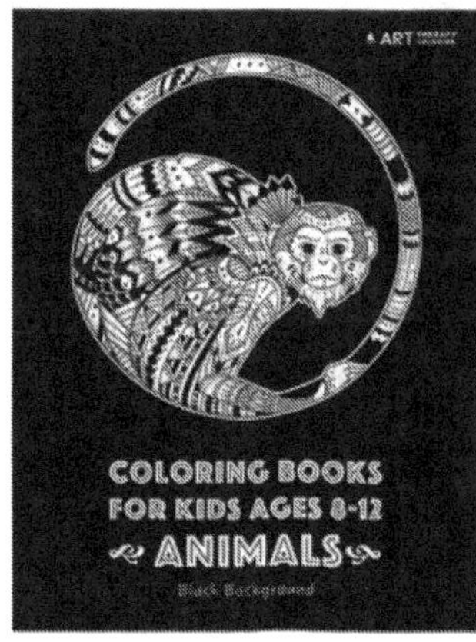
COLORING BOOKS
FOR KIDS AGES 8-12
ANIMALS
Black Background

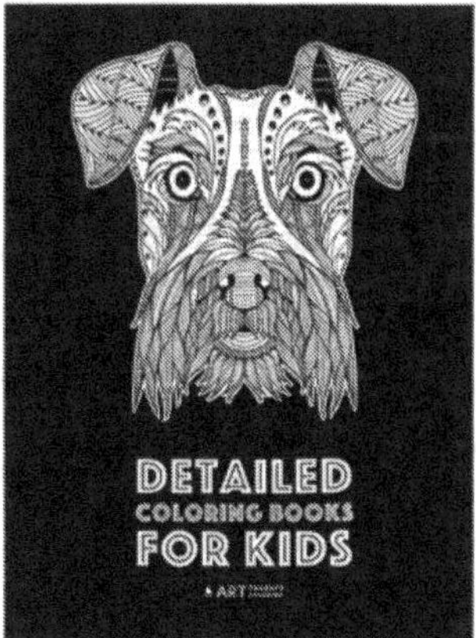
DETAILED
COLORING BOOKS
FOR KIDS

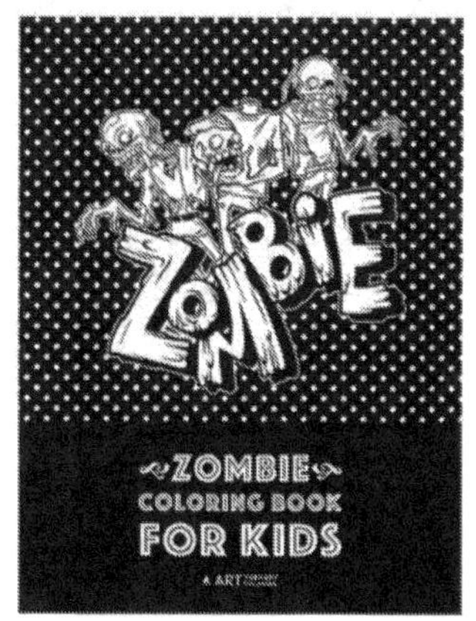
ZOMBIE
ZOMBIE
COLORING BOOK
FOR KIDS

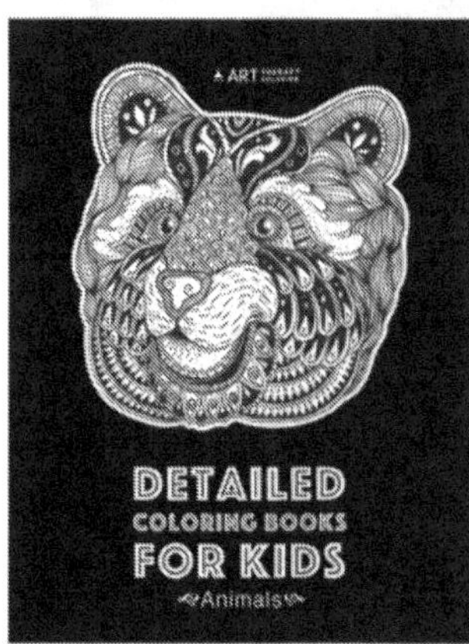
DETAILED
COLORING BOOKS
FOR KIDS
Animals

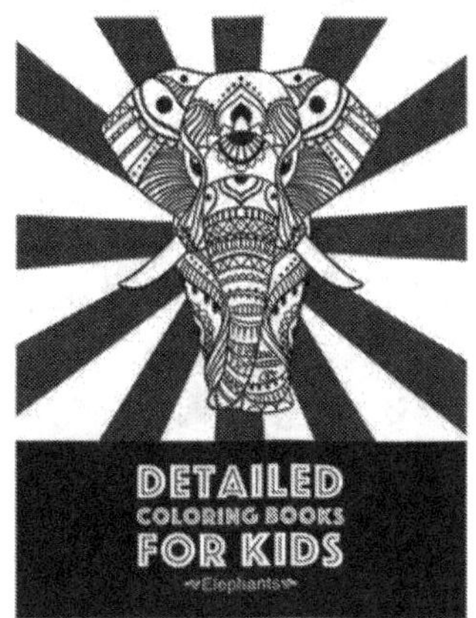
DETAILED
COLORING BOOKS
FOR KIDS
Elephants

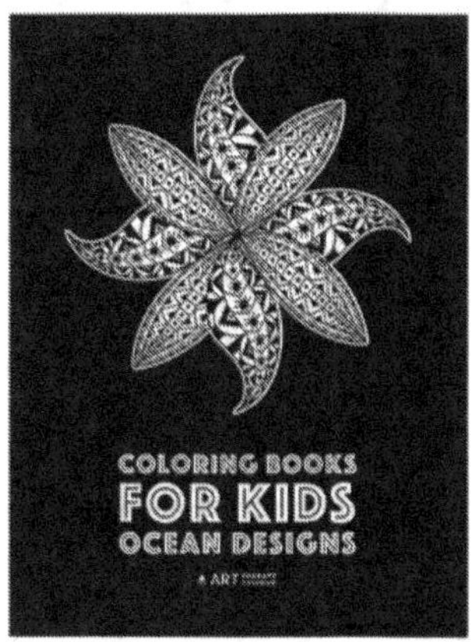
COLORING BOOKS
FOR KIDS
OCEAN DESIGNS

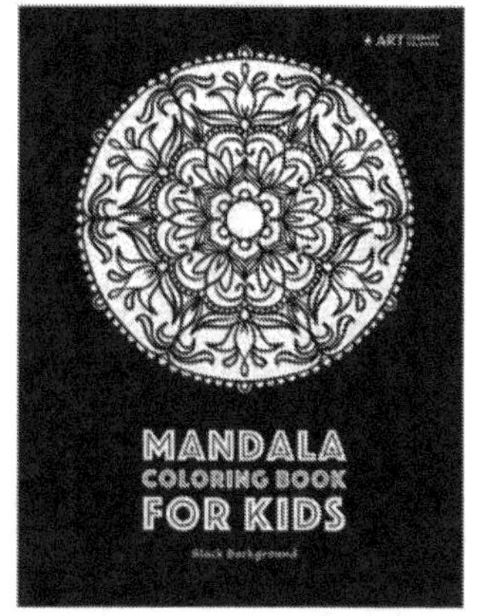
MANDALA
COLORING BOOK
FOR KIDS
Black Background

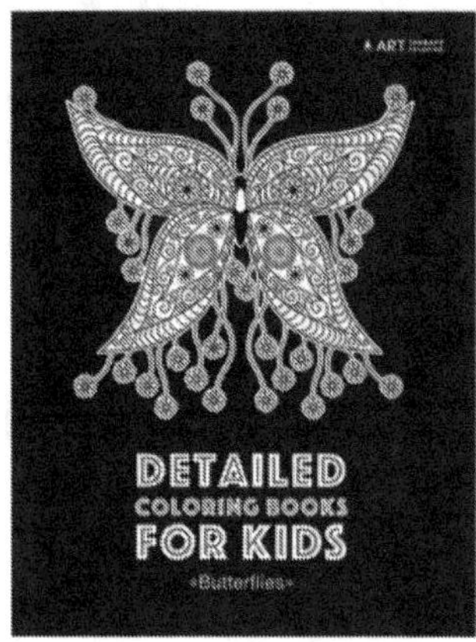
DETAILED
COLORING BOOKS
FOR KIDS
Butterflies

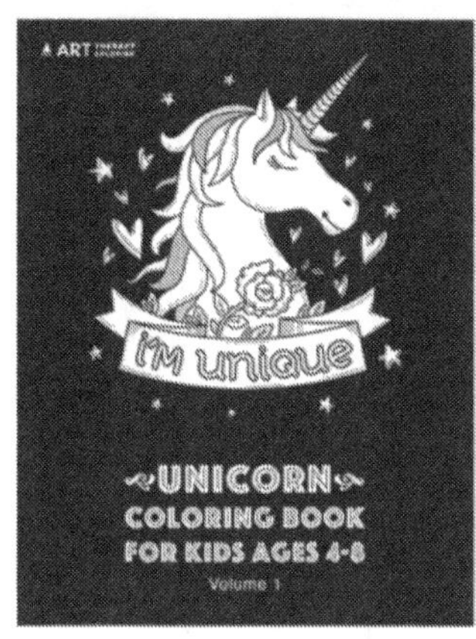
I'm unique
UNICORN
COLORING BOOK
FOR KIDS AGES 4-8
Volume 1

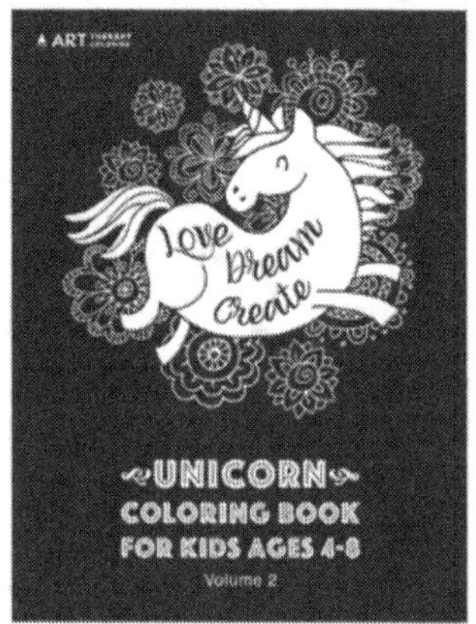
Love
Dream
Create
UNICORN
COLORING BOOK
FOR KIDS AGES 4-8
Volume 2

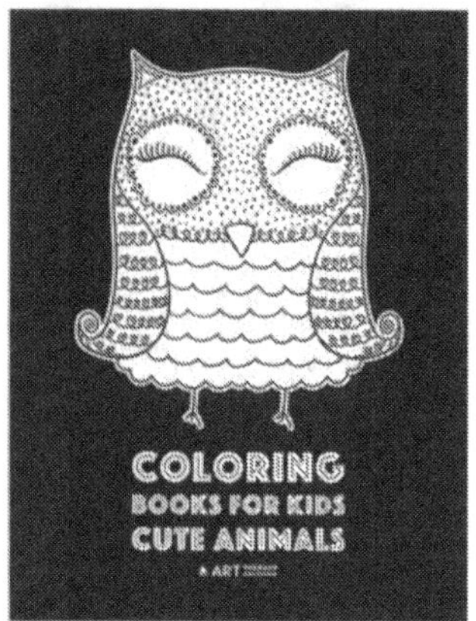
COLORING
BOOKS FOR KIDS
CUTE ANIMALS

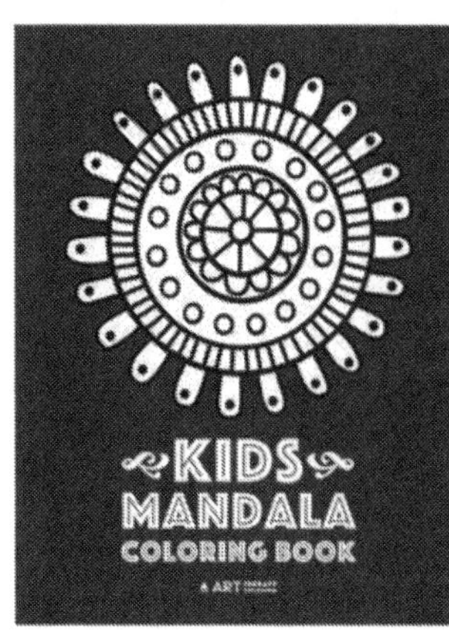
KIDS
MANDALA
COLORING BOOK

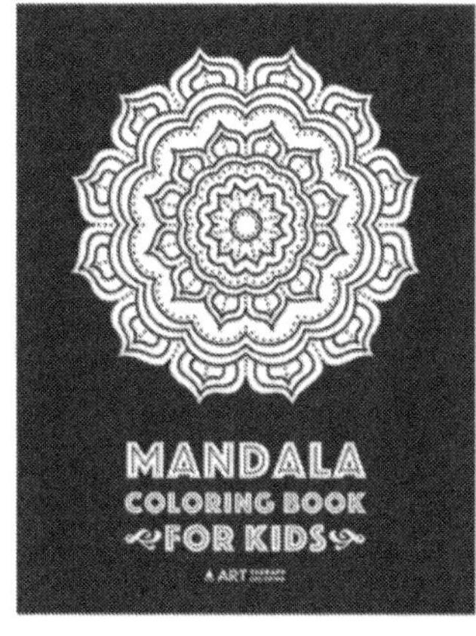
MANDALA
COLORING BOOK
FOR KIDS

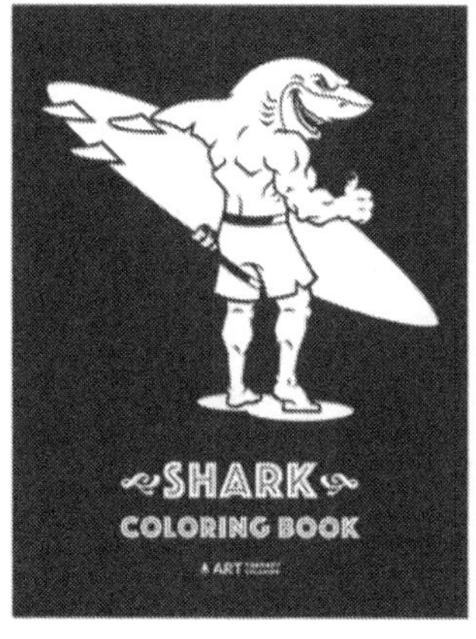
SHARK
COLORING BOOK

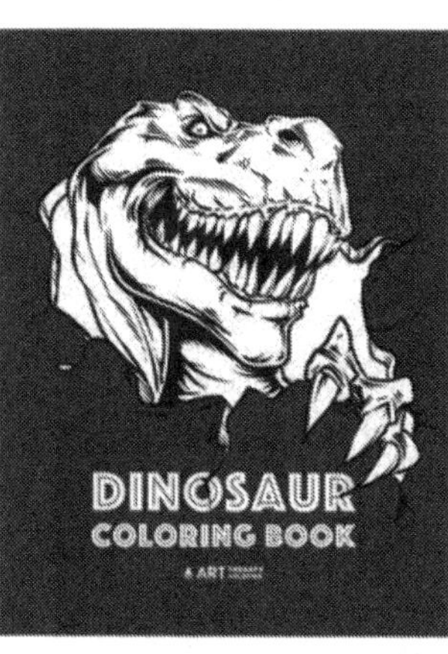
DINOSAUR
COLORING BOOK

Coloring Books For Special Occasions

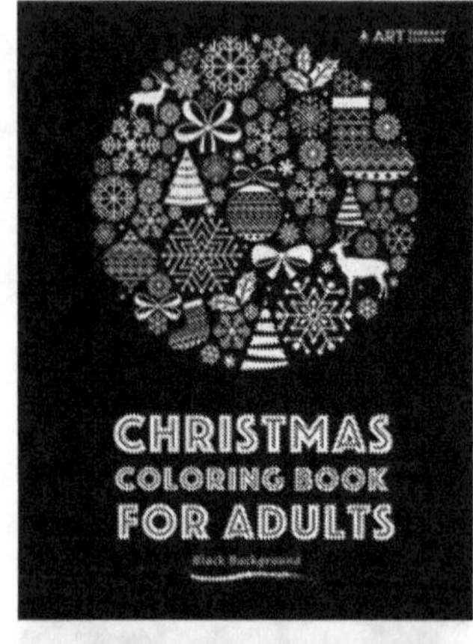
CHRISTMAS
COLORING BOOK
FOR ADULTS
Black Background

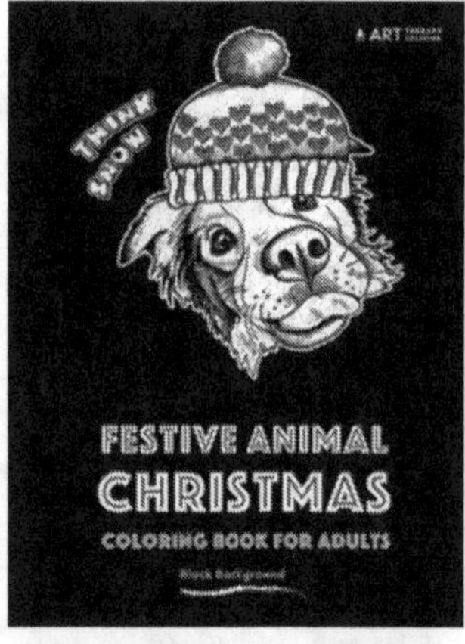
FESTIVE ANIMAL
CHRISTMAS
COLORING BOOK FOR ADULTS
Black Background

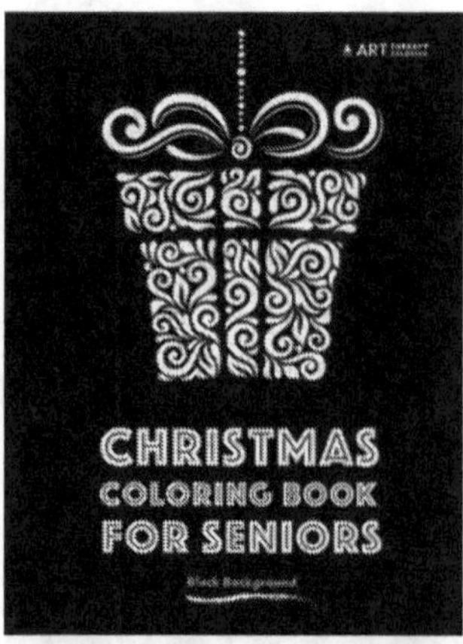
CHRISTMAS
COLORING BOOK
FOR SENIORS
Black Background

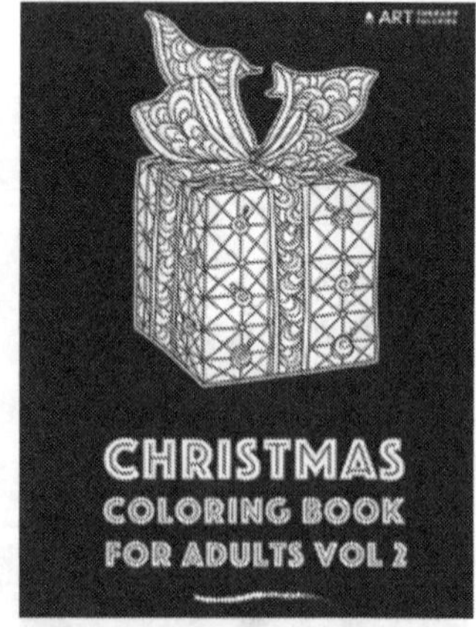
CHRISTMAS
COLORING BOOK
FOR ADULTS VOL 2

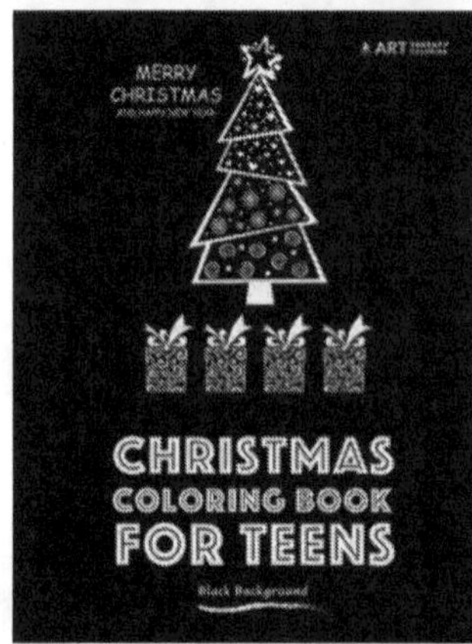
MERRY
CHRISTMAS
CHRISTMAS
COLORING BOOK
FOR TEENS
Black Background

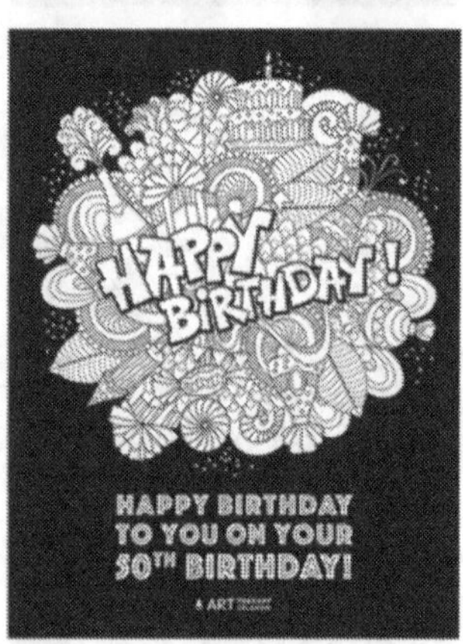
HAPPY BIRTHDAY!
HAPPY BIRTHDAY
TO YOU ON YOUR
50TH BIRTHDAY!

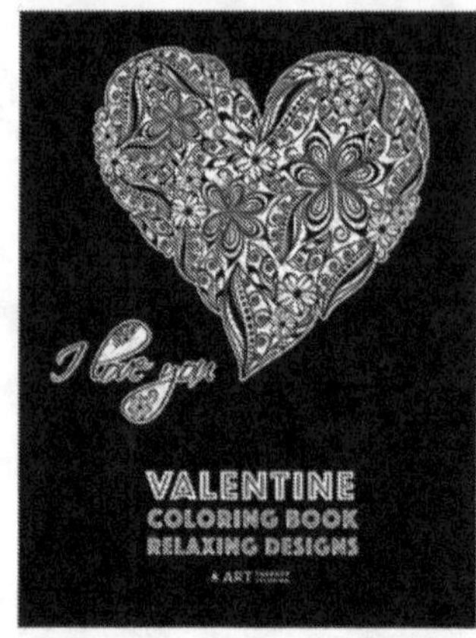
I love you
VALENTINE
COLORING BOOK
RELAXING DESIGNS

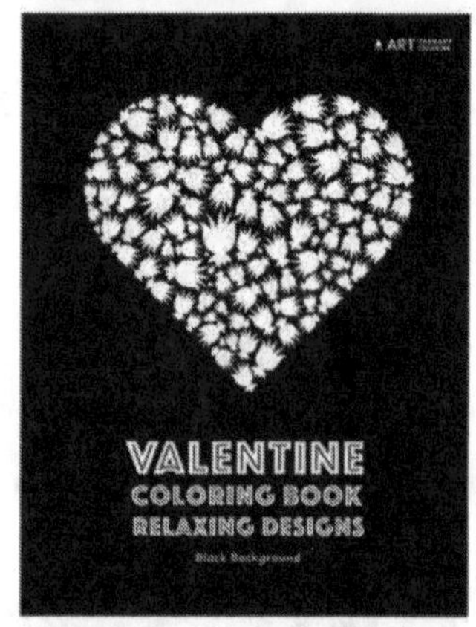
VALENTINE
COLORING BOOK
RELAXING DESIGNS
Black Background

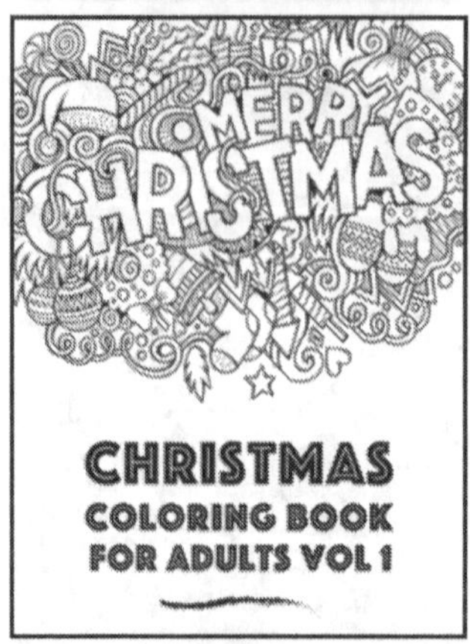
MERRY CHRISTMAS
CHRISTMAS
COLORING BOOK
FOR ADULTS VOL 1

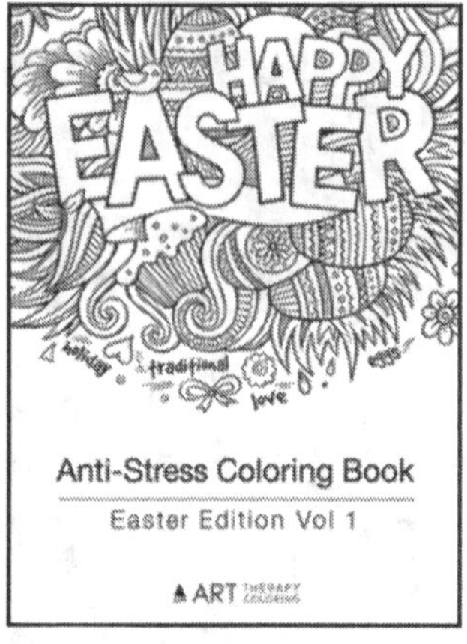
HAPPY EASTER
Anti-Stress Coloring Book
Easter Edition Vol 1
ART

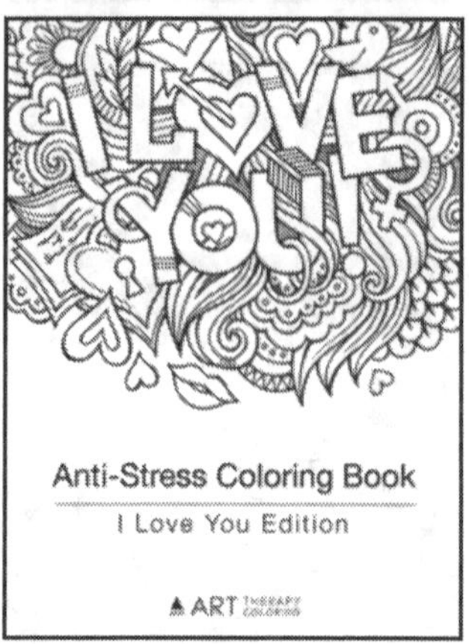
I LOVE YOU!
Anti-Stress Coloring Book
I Love You Edition
ART

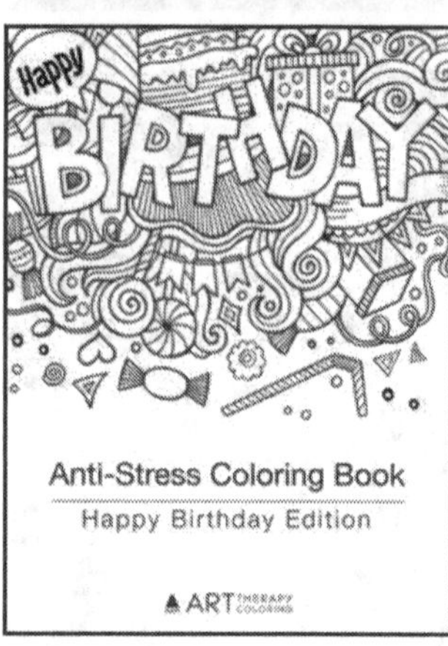
Happy BIRTHDAY
Anti-Stress Coloring Book
Happy Birthday Edition
ART

Coloring Book For Seniors
Anti-Stress Designs Vol 1

Published by:
Art Therapy Coloring
El Dorado Hills, California
www.arttherapycoloring.com

ISBN: 978-1-944427-25-2

www.ingramcontent.com/pod-product-compliance
Lightning Source LLC
LaVergne TN
LVHW080925110826
845155LV00039B/208

* 9 7 8 1 9 4 4 4 2 7 2 5 2 *